Untethered Marketing: The Role of the Cloud and Mobile Communications

John P. Foley, Jr.

10/5/2018

ISBN 978-0-615-75848

"We truly live in an untethered world, and far too many businesses are still stuck in a static, tethered environment that is not nearly nimble, flexible or visible enough to be successful in today's dynamic world"

Acknowledgements

Bear with me as I have a lot of people to thank here!

First, I would like to thank the many folks that saw me through this book. I truly couldn't have done it without you. To those who may have noticed that my mind was preoccupied at times and thought I was ignoring them: I wasn't ignoring you, you just may not have known that I was writing this book. Thank you for your patience and understanding! An immense amount of gratitude to everyone who contributed, edited, read and reread, proofed and designed this book. Even if your work was not chosen or edited in final production, your contribution is greatly appreciated.

I would like to thank each and every one of my employees at interlinkONE and Grow Socially, past and present, who come to work day in and day out and give all they have to grow the company. I'm fortunate to have such an amazing team.

To my wife Melanie, and my boys, Matthew, Trevor and Luke, who sacrifice some time with me (although sometimes I don't think they miss me); Thank you and love you!

Thank you to my colleague and advisor Cary Sherburne who continuously helps me "get 'er done".

To my friends and family who laugh with me, at me, but most importantly support me in all aspects of life… there are too many of you to list here, I'm grateful that there are so many of you!

For all of the professional colleagues that spend time with me including, but not limited to, Joe, Ken, Adam, Eric, Peter, Margie, Karen, and Barb, thank you all for your support.

Please forgive me for anyone's name I have failed to mention here. It means nothing more than that I'm becoming mildly forgetful! Thank you all for your efforts, encouragement and support!

Finally, to my Dad, this one's for you. I am grateful for the opportunities you and Mom have given me. See my note below:

> Hey Dad,
> Thank you, I love you,
> – John

How to Connect

Thank you very much for taking the time to read this book. If you have some free time, I'd love to chat with about marketing, this book or anything else, feel free to send me a note. You can reach me on Twitter at http://Twitter.com/JohnFoleyJr.

Mobilized Page created by http://www.iFlyMobi.com

Through out the book you will find QR Codes,
scan each one to receive enhanced content.

Foreword

Marketing. Ask 10 people for a working definition and you will likely get 10 different answers. One thing is for sure, though: Marketing is changing and the changes are dramatic and permanent.

Increasingly, more of everything we do is mobile. How we connect with others, engage, discuss, dialogue, bank, shop, compare and converse is now done on the go. This fact has not been lost on marketers, many of whom are trying to make sense of this new phenomenon and are looking for ways to leverage this undeniable trend.

John Foley is no stranger to these emerging trends. In fact, his expertise in business transformation is found at the intersection of marketing and technology. Who better then to lead us on our journey of discovery about the many advantages of mobile marketing?

In this book, John helps make sense of the opportunities and challenges inherent in the new wave of marketing applications. His "next generation" thinking is here on full display and is offered in a way that is actionable and scalable for business leaders, irrespective of size or scope.

If you are in any segment of the communications and/or marketing services business, you have found an outstanding resource. So go ahead, dive in. Get ready to leave ordinary behind and move to a higher level of understanding and opportunity. Step one in your business transformation begins now.

— Joseph P. Truncale, Ph.D.
President and CEO, NAPL

Untethered Marketing:
The Role of the Cloud and Mobile Communications

John P. Foley, Jr.

Table of Contents

Table of Figures

Chapter One: Operating Untethered

Untether: to release from a tether: to untether a horse
Tether: to fasten or confine with as if with a tether[1]

Just about everywhere you turn these days, someone is talking about, advertising, using, planning or in some way involved in mobile communications and/or cloud-based computing. Do you have an Apple iPad or Kindle Fire? Or a smartphone? Is your company using hosted software services—often called Software as a Service (SaaS)—for CRM (such as Salesforce.com), business intelligence (Business Objects) or other critical business processes? If so, you are already operating untethered to some extent. You have removed the tether that ties you to your desk, your server room, a fixed location, a fixed set of resources.

This is the way of the future - and the future is now. Are you on board? If not, what's holding you up? If you are confused about the whole cloud computing thing, or you just feel like you don't have enough information about where this is going and how to leverage untethered marketing techniques, you've come to the right place.

This book will provide you with insight, guidance, ideas, tips and hints for untethering your business and your marketing efforts. It's the way the world is going—and it is going quickly. Even the U.S. government has found that a quarter of its computing can be untethered—moved to the cloud—mostly because they are using less than 30% of all of their installed computing power. That's expensive waste! In fact, the U.S. government estimates that of its $80 billion in total IT spending, $20 billion can be moved to the cloud.[2]

---

[1]Dictionary.com

[2]*Federal Cloud Computing Strategy*, by VivekKundra, U.S. Chief Information Officer, February 8, 2011.

Not everything needs to be done via mobile communications or cloud computing, of course. But the more you can move into that realm, the more flexible and scalable your business will be. And even if you personally are still tethered, your marketing efforts must be as untethered as possible. If someone visits your web site from a smartphone, what will they see? A mobile-optimized web site or some big old generic website that is virtually impossible to navigate on the small screen? If the latter, you will lose them—it is a hassle to try to navigate and people just don't have the patience. They will look elsewhere for whatever it is they are looking for, and you will lose out.

For these and other reasons, companies are migrating more of their IT budgets to technologies that are reshaping the IT industry, including smartphones, media tablets, mobile networks, social networking and big data analytics. In a December 2011 forecast, IDC[3] predicted that worldwide IT spending would grow 6.9% year over year, with as much as 20% of this total spending driven by these disruptive technologies. The same study called 2012 the Year of Mobile Ascendency as mobile devices surpassed PCs in both shipments and spending, and mobile apps generated more revenue than the mainframe market.

The good news is that, whether you are a business or a consumer, it is easier than ever before to take advantage of these disruptive technologies and to be untethered. It is easier to accommodate the needs of customers and prospects across a variety of communication channels regardless of how they wish to communicate with you. It is also easier to work with a highly distributed and mobile workforce in productive and efficient ways.

A Nielsen[4] study reports that social networks and blogs now account for nearly a quarter of total time spent on the Internet in the U.S., with nearly four in five active Internet users visiting social networks and blogs. Increasingly, these users are accessing social media, blogs

---

[3]International Data Corporation – which provides market intelligence on IT, telecom and consumer technology industries

[4]*State of the Media: The Social Media Report,* Q32011, Nielsen.

and other Internet content with mobile devices. And it's not just the Millennials (Generation Y) either. The study also reported that Internet users over the age of 55 are driving the growth of social networking through the mobile Internet. Overall, nearly two in five social media users access these services from their mobile phones.

Perhaps one of the most telling signs of this dramatic transformation in business and consumer communications is reflected in a November 2011 report from eBay. The company expects $8 billion in mobile sales in 2012, up from $5 billion projected for 2011. eBay reports more than 50 million downloads of its mobile applications globally. CEO John Donahoe said, "We're now seeing a profound change in how consumers are behaving, and we are going to see more changes in the next three years than we've seen in the previous twenty in terms of shopping and payments." [5]

Echoing these sentiments, *Direct Marketing* Newsprojected that according to an IBM Coremetrics Benchmark Industry Report, 15% of e-Commerce shoppers will have logged onto brand websites using a mobile device during the 2011 holiday season.[6] Other experts expect to see mobile technology account for 20% or more of online traffic and sales by the 2012 holiday shopping season.

If you happen to subscribe to *Mobile Commerce Daily* (it's free, and you should), you will see daily articles about how well-known brands like JC Penney, Target, Kohl's and others are leveraging QR codes, mobile coupons, location-based services (LBS), and even near field communications (NFC) to make the consumer shopping experience seamless. If you aren't clear about QR codes, LBS or NFC, no worries. We'll talk in detail about those, too.

Some of the information in this book might be basic for you if you have already dabbled in the untethered world or are fairly well-established. Just skip over those parts—there is plenty more here

---

[5] *eBay expects $5B in mobile sales in 2011,* by Rimma Kats, Mobile Commerce Daily, November 7, 2011.

[6] *IBM: 15% of online holiday shopping will be done on mobile devices,* by Juan Martinez, Direct Marketing News, November 4, 2011

for you to use, even if you have already stepped into mobile/cloud computing and communications.

So here's the scoop: we'll start by laying down some of the basics so everyone is on the same page. Then we will get into details about how to use these basics to jump-start your business. You may be surprised to find that it is easier and more affordable than you think to be an untethered marketer. Heck, this is even an untethered book, in a way. We have a special resource web site set up at UntetheredMarketing.com that extends the value of the book and keeps it current in this rapidly changing world. You can subscribe to our newsletter, comment on our blog, and tell us your stories. We're anxious to get the conversation going!

In the next chapter, we will define cloud computing in layman's terms, include a discussion of pros and cons, and explain why now is the time to take advantage of the cloud. It will include a discussion about security and give examples from various industries of how cloud computing can reduce costs and improve performance. I will share experiences from my companies, interlinkONE, Grow Socially and iFlyMobi, not all of which are pretty, especially when we got started in the mid-1990s. And I will share stories from others as well.

Today, we're managing Fortune 500 businesses online, in the cloud, including financial data from investment companies. That was harder to do 10 or 15 years ago, and I'll tell you why.

When we first started interlinkONE, we used to talk to potential customers about the value and benefits of an end-to-end marketing automation solution. This solution could meet their multichannel communications, fulfillment and kitting requirements for prospectuses and other critical applications a financial services company needed. It was hard enough to sell the solution in the first place. Once you convinced them that they could benefit from marketing automation, the next thing you had to do was sell them on the Applications Service Provider (ASP) model, a predecessor to cloud computing. We actually got into the business before the term "ASP" was invented, which made it even more difficult to sell this unique model. If you made it through those hoops and got the buy-in from the business leader or the VP of Marketing, the next hurdle was the company's IT department. Back in those days, the late 1990s, when you explained to the average corporate IT professional that you operated via the Internet, delivering services from a shared data center, many of them looked at you as though you had two heads. In many cases, they were focused on building their own internal IT fiefdom and had no interest in using outside services.

The concept of an ASP was not really new, though. One could argue that it was a descendent of the service bureaus of the 1960s and 1970s that were established to allow companies to take advantage of shared mainframe computing. According to *Inc. Magazine*, JosteinEikeland, the founder of TeleComputing, a company that provides outsourced computing and consulting services in Northern Europe, is credited with coining the acronym ASP in 1996, but it took a while for the term to come into popular usage.

If you could get through all the hoops, including convincing IT to support the concept, you then had to implement and maintain the service. We were dependent upon shared data centers for computing resources. Remember, this is during the dot-com bubble in the late 1990s. Investors such as CMGI, founded by David Wetherell and Breakaway Solutions (which ceased operations in 2002 after filing bankruptcy), were investing like crazy in Internet-related companies that basically had no revenues. NaviSite, Engage, Lycos—those are just a few of the names you may remember from that era. For many of these Internet-based companies, including mine, using a shared data center made a lot of sense rather than investing in building your own. But it came with risks.

You can think of these large data centers, like the ones operated by NaviSite, UUNet and Exodus, as "data hotels." There is room for people to come in and live there with their equipment, taking advantage of the infrastructure that was already in place and could be shared by multiple tenants. And they were building these centers at a rapid pace. People were literally throwing money their way. The concept was solid, but the timing was wrong. The business model was flawed. You don't build hotels if you don't have customers to occupy them. There should be a plan to roll out increased capacity as the volume grows. Those were crazy times, though, and everyone was caught up in a frenzy, believing that the world had changed forever and they were leading the charge. In a way, they were. Early adopters often take a lot of arrows; some make it and some don't. I used to go into these facilities and there was no one there, yet these guys were making money hand over fist and their stock was going through the roof.

CMGI, an investor in NaviSite where we hosted our solution, is a good example of what was going on back then. Lucky for them, NaviSite survived. Many others did not. CMGI went public in 1994 and its stock boomed during the dot-com bubble, peaking at $163 in 2000, with a market capitalization of more than $40 billion.[7] When the bubble burst, CMGI's stock tumbled, falling below $1 in 2002. By 2006, the company's market capitalization was $662 million. They were certainly not alone. Where did all that money go? It's a mind-boggling period in the world's financial history.

So there we were, in the middle of all of this. In those days, we had to acquire hardware, set it up, ship it to the data center, and go there to get it set up. Then, as these data centers started going out of business, it was a scramble to find a new data center partner, move all our stuff, and do this without interrupting customer services. I'm lucky I have any hair left!

Today, it is totally different. Cloud computing and the concept of outsourcing computing services and applications are becoming much more accepted. Capabilities like virtual machines or virtual servers, which we will talk more about in Chapter Two, make it fast and easy to bring up new applications and new customers. The data centers or cloud computing service providers are big names that are much more stable, have real revenues, and for the most part, don't depend solely

---

[7]www.Wikipedia.com, August 16, 2012

on providing "data hotels" for their survival. The sales process for us is easier, too. You are starting from a different knowledge level and level of acceptance of the business model, from the C-Suite through Operations and IT. In a nutshell, operating an untethered business is an achievable reality today, one that your business can readily take advantage of.

So with that as a backdrop, if you are still cloudy on cloud computing, Chapter Two should take care of that, and give you ideas about how you can leverage this technology to streamline your own business.

In Chapter Three, we will turn our attention to mobile computing and mobile marketing. This will include a mobile communications overview, including smartphones, tablets, their adoption rates, and definitions of things such as near field communications (NFC), QR codes, augmented reality, location-based services (LBS), mobile wallet, geo-fencing and more.

Clearly mobile communications—and mobile marketing—are growth areas, and we will share the most current data as of this writing. If you haven't already bought into the whole mobile thing, you will by the end of the chapter. This is not hype. It is fact. The plethora of mobile communications devices out there, the increasing bandwidth, and the growing availability of useful, helpful, and even fun "apps" for

these devices will continue to push that growth, as well as behavioral changes for businesses and for consumers of all ages.

We'll talk about the various operating systems for mobile devices—Apple, Android, and Blackberry being the primary ones—and suggest where your focus should be.

We'll introduce the concept of the mobile web. We'll also delve into social media and talk about how mobile is changing that landscape as well. We'll talk about the tools that will help you be a more effective mobile marketer and how these tools will help you create content once and automatically repurpose it for the multitude of devices out there.

Understanding the mobile landscape is one of the most important aspects of untethering your marketing strategies.

Chapter Four is titled "There's an App for That," and you've likely heard that phrase before. In Chapter Four, we will unravel the mystery of "apps," applications that are specifically designed for mobile devices, including tablets and smartphones. What are they, how do you build them, how do you get them out into the world? We'll untangle the web of confusion around the various "app stores," including the Apple App Store, Android Marketplace, Amazon, Apple's iTunes, and more. We'll talk about how or whether you should charge for these apps. We will also make clear the difference between web applications and mobile apps and discuss the differences between tablet and smartphone deployments.

This chapter, building on the previous chapters, will get you geared up for mobile, and will also help you understand the synergy between mobile communications, marketing and other media, including web, print and broadcast.

By the time we get to Chapter Five, we have covered the basic ground you need to understand in order to untether your business. Chapter Five will give you a view of the completely untethered business of the future. It will go more in depth into exactly how companies are using the cloud and mobile communications today, and what that might mean for the future. What are the issues with privacy? How will the workforce be affected? How can you effectively integrate mobile/remote workers into the mix? We'll give you tips and hints for managing in this very different environment.

The business of the future will be an untethered business. In some cases, depending on the nature of the business, you may not even need a bricks and mortar headquarters. In most cases, those headquarters facilities will be much more compact and the mobile workforce can even be globally dispersed. The end result is a very different picture of the business of the future than we are used to thinking about today. For many companies, this will be a difficult transition. But on the flip side, there are many companies, large and small, that are already operating virtually, and doing it well. Your challenge will be to find the happy medium that will allow you to take your business to a new level.

In Chapter Six, we will build on what we have already discussed in terms of social media. This is an area that is difficult to cover in print, since it changes so quickly. That's where our resource web site will come in handy. We collect the latest information there so you can stay current.

Chapter Six will talk about the modern media mix and how social media fits in. It will cover concepts such as crowd sourcing and viral marketing. It will provide you with the latest status of the most popular social media venues and give you statistics on how people are using them—from both a business and a personal perspective. It is important to understand both sides, since many of your customers are using these sites on a regular basis, and for many, it can be the best way to not only reach them, but to engage them in a meaningful, ongoing dialog.

A critical element of your untethered business strategy is an untethered marketing plan, and that's what we will discuss in Chapter Seven. One of my companies, Grow Socially, is actively engaged with a number of clients in building and deploying these marketing strategies. We will leverage that real-world work to bring you ideas that you can put to work in your own business. This will include detailed work plans that can be incorporated into your company's overall marketing strategy.

Finally, in Chapter Eight, we will delve into where we go from here. We'll talk about what we can expect to see in terms of developments over the next few years and what those developments likely mean for your business. We will talk about the importance of having a formal, written business plan and give you examples and guidelines for developing one if you don't already have one in place. We'll talk about setting specific goals and ROI targets.

By the end of Chapter Eight, you will be ready to embark upon your untethered strategy and break out the old way of thinking.

And in Chapter Nine, we will do what all good business books do—wrap it all up with a nice bow, including a summary of the questions you need to ask yourself and the steps you need to take to ensure a healthy, robust and successful untethered business far into the future.

Adapting to change and transforming your business can be difficult, but both are essential for business success in a digital world. Challenging? Certainly. It's not easy, but it is easier than it has ever been before. Exciting? Absolutely. Rife with opportunity. It's a chance to really unleash your creativity and that of your people. And a more intimate relationship with customers than you ever dreamed possible.

So let's dive in, get our heads into the clouds, and make sure we have a good understanding of what people mean by cloud computing!

Scan to receive a can't miss white paper on QR codes!

Chapter Two: Cloud Computing Made Simple

Are you a little "cloudy" about what is meant by cloud computing? If so, you are not alone. Nonetheless, you can hardly read the news, turn on the TV or open a magazine without encountering the terms "cloud computing" or "in the cloud" being bandied about by some talking head, columnist, expert or advertisement. These voices are usually accompanied by images of clouds and an assumption that everyone knows what "The Cloud" means. If you understand cloud computing, feel free to skip this chapter, which is a cloud computing primer. Don't worry, it won't get boringly technical. And we'll also talk about a related concept, software as a service (SaaS) and how that is different from cloud computing.

According to Wikipedia,[8] "Cloud computing is the delivery of computing as a service rather than a product, whereby shared resources, software, and information are provided to computers and other devices as a utility (like the electricity grid) over a network (typically the Internet). The name is actually a metaphor for the Internet, which is often depicted in technical diagrams as a cloud. But there is more to it than that.

Cloud computing is distinguished by the way services are delivered. Forrester defines a "cloud" as "a standardized IT capability (services, software or infrastructure) delivered in a pay-per-use, self-service way."[9]

Figure 1. Cloud Computing

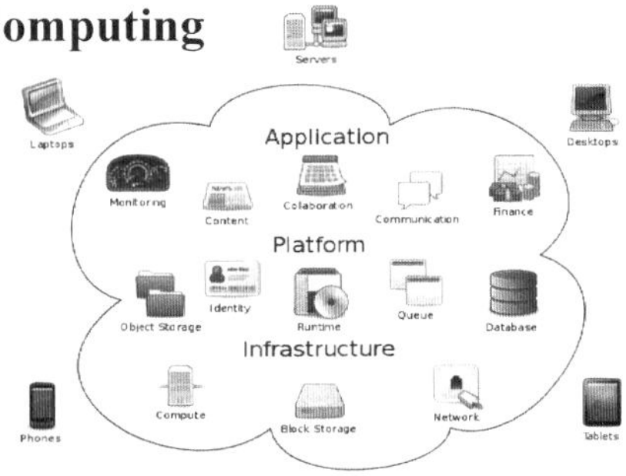

Cloud Computing

---

[8]www.Wikipedia.com, November 2, 2011

[9]http://www.forrester.com/TechRadar+For+Infrastructure+Operations+Professionals+Cloud+Computing+Q4+2011/fulltext/-/E-RES60916

Figure 1. Source: Wikipedia, November 2, 2011

Consider that the Internet began to gain business and consumer acceptance in 1995, marked by the highly publicized Netscape IPO that caught the market's attention and began the migration of many things to this "network of networks". The Internet, often called "the web" (short for worldwide web) is now nearing the two-decade mark in terms of general public awareness. It has become ubiquitous, around the globe. Even in emerging economies such as the BRIC (Brazil, Russia, India, China) and MIST (Mexico, Indonesia, South Korea and Turkey) countries, while online penetration may be lower than the U.S. and other developed countries, consumers and businesses are rapidly adopting smartphones and tablets, giving them access to the Internet and leapfrogging the need to have or have access to a PC to take advantage of all of the resources available via the web. This is an important trend because, especially in developing countries, it can be easier to afford a smartphone than a PC. The smartphone also serves as a phone, giving users a multifunctional device that keeps them in touch with friends, family, news, video, games, weather, books and more. These users are truly untethered and will increasingly rely on cloud-based applications to simplify their online experience.

These devices are a good example of how cloud computing is being used by consumers as well as businesses. While they have an amazing amount of storage, it is not unlimited. Users need the ability to offload some portion of their data as well as the ability to back up that data. When you buy an iPhone, you can automatically back it up to the cloud. Apple gives you a certain amount of space free, and you pay for additional storage. Rather than having to connect your phone to your computer to back up data, music, photos, email and anything else you may have on the phone, you can now do it automatically with wireless or 3G connectivity. By the end of this chapter, you will understand (if you don't already) that Apple simply spins up new capacity as new customers come online, whether they are using the free or the paid service.

Another example is Amazon's Kindle Fire, which we will talk about in more detail in Chapter Three during our tablet computing discussion. Its slick interface presents a "carousel" to users that shows them everything they have in their library, from books to video, from music to apps. Users can choose to display the entire library (whether or not it is physically loaded onto the device), view items by category, or view only the items that are physically on the device. A user might choose to remove a book from the device once it has been read, but it is still available in perpetuity in the cloud and can easily be downloaded if it is needed again. The user can either leave it on the carousel or choose to remove it from the carousel to have a more uncluttered view. As with Apple, a certain amount of storage is provided for free, and additional storage is available for a fee if it is needed.

There is no question that we are in the mobile (untethered!) age.

A recent Ad Age article[10] reports that in the U.S., online penetration stands at 69%; mobile phone usage at 50%; and smartphone usage at 31% (with another 25% planning to buy in the next 12 months). It also found that 62% of the most tech-engaged population segment is likely to buy a new computer or tablet in the next 18 months.

The economic impact of the web cannot be overemphasized. McKinsey Global Institute issued a May 2011 report[11] stating that on average, the Internet contributes 3.4% to GDP in the 13 countries covered by the research, an amount the size of Spain or Canada in terms of GDP, and growing at a faster rate than Brazil. And the Internet accounted for 21% of GDP growth over the last five years among the developed countries studied. According to the study, the Internet is also a catalyst for job creation, stating, "Among 4,800 small and medium-size enterprises surveyed, the Internet created 2.6 jobs for each lost to technology-related efficiencies." The report warns that companies should pay attention to how quickly Internet technologies can disrupt business models by radically changing markets and driving

---

[10] *Stat of the Day: How Emerging Markets Do Mobile*, by Matt Carmichael, AdAge.com, Published November 1, 2011

[11] *Internet matter: The Net's sweeping impact on growth, jobs and prosperity*, McKinsey Global Institute, May 2011

efficiencies. Cloud computing and mobile communications are just two of the Internet-related disruptive technologies that are driving radical change.

The web has become integral to many activities for consumers as well as businesses. From seeking information about products and services prior to purchasing, to online banking, staying current with the news, streaming video and gaming and social media, the everyday consumer is finding more and more uses for rapid-fire internet technologies. Increasingly, businesses are turning to the cloud to host business applications or to utilize web-based tools and/or mobile apps that can access the cloud from desktops and mobile devices. These applications or tools, and the data associated with them, reside in remote shared data centers rather than on servers located on-site at the enterprise (inside the firewall) as has been the custom in the past. Wikipedia points out, "This type of data center environment allows enterprises to get their applications up and running faster, with easier manageability and less maintenance, and enables IT to more rapidly adjust IT resources (such as servers, storage, and networking) to meet fluctuating and unpredictable business demand." It can also reduce—but not eliminate—the IT staffing requirement on-site.

For on-site installations, experts are reluctant to quote the ratio of IT staff required per server because of the many variables from one installation to another. But Microsoft states that in a typical server environment in a small- to mid-sized business, one IT FTE[12] can manage 4.6 servers, estimating that the labor to manage a single server costs about $23,807 annually.[13] This is above and beyond the cost of the server itself (including energy), software licenses, software maintenance, and the need to periodically upgrade, repair or replace servers.

---

[12]FTE = full-time equivalent

[13]*Server Infrastructure Optimization: Best Practices to Reduce IT Operational Costs*, Microsoft, January 2009.

Cloud Computing Deployment Models

Deployment models for cloud computing include:

- Public cloud, where resources are provisioned on a self-service basis via the Internet from an off-site third-party provider who bills based on computing usage.
- Community cloud, featuring an infrastructure that is shared among several organizations that share similar concerns. This model spreads costs across a smaller base than the public cloud, but a larger base than a private cloud.
- Private cloud, operated solely for a single organization, and can be managed internally or hosted externally by a third-party provider.
- Hybrid cloud joins together two or more clouds of the types described above. Each remains a unique entity but they are connected in a manner that makes it easy to move programs and data from one system to another.

One historical barrier to adoption of cloud computing has been a concern about security and privacy. This includes potential access of private data by unauthorized third parties (or hackers), as well as the potential for the hosting entity to monitor activity (and data) on their servers. Reputable providers of cloud computing have aggressive security measures in place and are serious about regulatory compliance, where appropriate, by complying with HIPAA, SOX, SAS 70 certification and other relevant regulatory and compliance models. While security breaches at providers of cloud services are high profile news stories, they are actually quite rare.

Another barrier is simply resistance to change. Think about the travails of RIM, once a mobile leader with its Blackberry family of products. Notwithstanding its global outage in 2011, I believe that the real reason RIM got into trouble and began losing significant market share to the Apple and Android operating systems is because of the requirement for a dedicated, proprietary Blackberry server and operation within its own proprietary network. When Blackberry was really the only option for a mobile business communications network, corporate IT departments were adopting right and left, and RIM was flying high. Corporate IT professionals liked the level of centralized control they had over the devices down to the minutest detail, enabled by the blend of RIM's operation in tandem with the BlackBerry Enterprise Server inside the corporate firewall. They were comfortable with its proprietary server, and perhaps had a false sense of security that this proprietary configuration could not be breached. They certainly didn't have the same level of comfort with iOS and Android as these devices began to emerge. Not that IT professionals didn't want to use them for their own personal use—many did. But they were certainly reluctant to risk having them raise havoc with their networks.

That all began to change with RIM's major outage in 2011, which reportedly started due to the failure of one of RIM's core switches and the subsequent failure of its redundant systems. The outage was exacerbated when RIM began throttling back service to Europe in an attempt to stabilize the situation. This, in turn, caused a backup of mail in other regions of the world that were trying to reach RIM's European customers.[14] In addition to growing demand from users for different communications options, this service outage served as a wake-up call to corporations who were so dependent on their Blackberry networks to conduct business, raising significant questions about the future health of RIM's network and its ability to scale. It also raised questions about the advisability of depending on a third-party proprietary network for these mission critical applications and activities.

RIM's demise was initially delayed by the power of the IT fiefdoms. What I mean by that is that we are all products of our environment. IT departments were very comfortable with RIM and resisted approval of iPhones and Android-based phones being used on the corporate network despite the flood of help desk requests many were receiving.

---

[14]*BlackBerry's Latest Outage Caused by Huge Email Backup*, by Lance Ulanoff, Mashable.com, October 12, 2011.

BlackBerry is what they knew best, and it is natural to resist new technologies, even for IT people. They stand by what they know works, and when you try to get them to change, it can be difficult. I sure found that when trying to sell the application service provider —and later the Software as a Service—model to corporate IT departments.

But what was different in the mobile phone arena was the groundswell of demand by employees that they be able to use their iPhones and Android phones in the workplace and on the corporate network. In fact, many employees were willing to purchase their own phones rather than using company-purchased phones if they could have an Android or iPhone. After a time, that became a force that could not be resisted. Users liked the fact that there wasn't a proprietary server in the middle of their connectivity with an iPhone, and they liked the ability to connect to a wide variety of email accounts. At the same time, iOS and Android phones began having the ability to partition devices to toggle between work and personal mode using applications such as AT&T's Toggle or BizzTrust for Android. Meanwhile, when you talked to a lot of the IT people, they were all caught up in bits and bytes, and not really thinking about user needs so much as they were focused on continuing with what had worked for them in the past.

This resistance on the part of IT departments, which seems to be fading—whether under pressure or through better education, I'm not sure—can also be a big problem for CEOs who would like to see some of these new technologies leveraged for business purposes, including the capabilities embodied in the iOS and Android operating systems for phones and tablets. Not only do we have to fight the resistance to change from the outside, there are internal struggles as well. Or worse, CEOs relied on the advice of an IT department that appeared to have preservation of its fiefdom as a primary goal, foregoing what might be game-changing technology advances for their companies.

The truth is that an individual corporate IT department can't guard against security breaches. I would even argue that cloud computing service providers do a better job of guarding against those breaches than a proprietary server can. In fact, 90% of businesses surveyed by the Ponemon Institute, a privacy research firm, reported having had one or more security breaches per year. So the whole security argument needs to be tossed out.

One other thing to consider, especially as you think about internally developed and maintained applications and services versus externally developed and maintained applications and services, is the need for flexibility and haste, especially in terms of keeping those applications, solutions and services updated to address regulatory compliance concerns and new capabilities. Just that one aspect can be a huge drain on an IT staff, while the cost of updates to a hosted solution are spread out over a large number of users, making these updates more affordable for everyone, and not creating a drain on the already overburdened corporate IT staff.

When considering these "barriers," you should consider how secure and reliable your internal servers actually are. I am known to challenge folks to let me try to hack into their servers and because of this I believe that for most organizations, especially small to mid-sized businesses, this would be much easier to accomplish than it would to hack into the server base of an operator of cloud-based services, such as Amazon, Google or Microsoft. Not that I would really try to hack into either, but I'm just sayin'. It is certainly food for thought. And you should also open your eyes to the enhanced business benefits cloud computing can bring. Some additional examples are provided below, in the Cloud Computing Examples section of this chapter.

I enjoy this comment from Harvard Business Review's Andrew McAfee, "If you will pardon the pun, the near-term forecast for corporate computing is only partly cloudy." But you shouldn't let that prevent you and your company from making some bold moves to try out these technologies. The only way to learn for yourself is to give it a shot. Again, I am not saying that everything belongs in the cloud. But cloud computing should play some role in any corporate computing environment.

And the world of cloud computing is certainly one of co-opetition (a combination of competition and cooperation in the effort to facilitate a win-win outcome)…there is no better example of that than Netflix stating it plans to rely on Amazon's cloud for years to come. These two bitter competitors have found a way to work together—at least on one level.

Virtual Servers

Another aspect of cloud computing is the concept of virtual servers or virtual machines. I don't want to get too far down into the weeds here, but this concept is important to understand, at least at a higher level. The term virtual server or virtual machine refers to a software implementation of a server that acts like a physical machine. A virtual server can be dedicated to a single application, or it can run a full operating system. Either way, the virtual server acts like a real server in the sense that it cannot break out of its boundaries. Examples of software that enable virtual servers are VMWare from EMC, Microsoft Virtual Server, Microsoft Hyper-V or the Xen cloud platform from Oracle.

VMWare initially wrote the book on server virtualization. The company was founded in 1998 and eventually acquired by EMC. It changed the computing game when it brought its first virtual server product to market in 2001.

Virtual servers are one reason that cloud computing is so cool. It can take significant time and investment to bring a new physical server online. You must purchase and install the server and associated physical hardware, add software, do testing…and if you are using a remote hosting service, you also need to haul or ship your servers there to be brought online. But with virtual computing in the cloud, you can bring up a virtual server in a matter of minutes without buying new hardware. You are simply leveraging a resource that is already there, buying more cloud computing capacity. You can also have servers in a "wait state." That means when that particular virtual machine is not required, everything stops. It is not using memory or other resources. When it is needed, there might be a nanosecond delay, but then it is running at full speed. In other words, virtual machines give you capacity on demand at all levels: hardware, software and virtual servers.

Virtual servers can run in any of the cloud computing models described above. Based on our experience, we recommend that you build a cluster of physical hosts rather than putting all your eggs in one basket—or on one server. If you fry the server, you are dead. But if you are working with a cluster server concept and you have a problem with one virtual server, another will pop up within seconds on another host in the cluster, with no interruption in service and no need to pull hardware or hard drives from the configuration. The cloud provider takes care of any of those issues. This capability has really helped move virtualization forward.

Cloud Computing Examples

One of the key benefits of cloud computing is the ability to scale up services on demand to accommodate peak processing needs or business growth. Perhaps even more important is the ability to quickly scale down the level of resources when necessary. Both are much more difficult to do when those resources are owned internally.

As I have said before, not everything can—or should—be placed in the cloud. Most applicable are services or infrastructure that can be delivered in a standardized pay-per-use self-service way that benefit from economies of scale—that is, distributing the cost of the computing resources across many clients, who each individually may wish to scale up and down at will. Here are some examples that might make this concept clearer.

NASDAQ Market Replay Service. If anyone should be concerned about security and privacy it is NASDAQ, a global stock exchange operating in 24 markets. One would think such a company would be leery of using the cloud, and it is for day-to-day operations. However, NASDAQ does use the cloud for its Market Replay service, a replay and analysis tool that allows users to view the consolidated order book and trade data for NASDAQ, the New York Stock Exchange (NYSE) and other regional exchange-listed securities at any point in time. Investors can use Market Replay, a subscription service, to help validate best execution and regulatory compliance. Brokers and traders can use the tool to reconstruct the events around their trade to determine whether there was a missed opportunity or an unforeseen event. Brokers can send clients a NASDAQ-validated screen shot of the moment their particular trade occurred, confirming the quality of the execution and reducing the number of customer inquiries. Data availability is delayed at least 15 minutes.

For NASDAQ, operating this service in the cloud allows them to make this valuable historical data available without compromising its trading operations during the day, better managing the volume of data and data manipulation required of its servers during trading hours and keeping real-time trade activities inside its firewall for added security.

United States Army. The U.S. Army is another organization that is highly conscious of—one might almost say paranoid about—security, but still uses the cloud for some applications. One of these is testing a troop vulnerability application, a process that requires the use of historical data and previous battle information. The application, once finalized, will not be hosted in the cloud. Using the cloud during the development and testing process allows the Army to verify the amount of computing power that will ultimately be needed—will they need a $25 million or a $50 million data center? That is a fairly wide spread that they would prefer to narrow down before investing in the actual data center hardware and facility. The cloud allows them to do that. This type of use of cloud computing—testing new applications—is becoming increasingly common as organizations seek to reduce investment risks.

Pathwork Diagnostics. This medical startup company specializes in cancer tissue analysis. Its process requires a massive data warehouse that hosts millions of samples of oncology tissue and respective DNA profiles. For new undiagnosed tissue samples, Pathwork Diagnostics does a DNA profile and compares it to all of the rest of the DNA samples they have in the database. Not only does this give them high predictability in terms of being able to diagnose the specific type of cancer, they can do so quickly. What used to take weeks in the past now can take as little as 24 hours. Although the application does not run in the cloud, Pathwork Diagnostics uses thousands of machines and terabytes of data in the cloud to build the data warehouse. Once it is built, it is downloaded to their own servers.

For a startup company, this reduces the required investment, saving them a huge amount of money. In this case, the cloud could be the difference between being able to get the business off the ground—or not.

In traditional computing models, it can take days or weeks to scale up capacity. By using the cloud, new capacity can be available in as little as 15 minutes. If you can build it, you can deploy it fast, and scale up quickly to meet demand, especially with use of virtualization as described above

The cloud and virtualization are also important elements of a business continuity strategy. Several years ago, when we were doing work for Cisco Systems, Cisco required that we have a redundant configuration on each side of the country using multiple Tier One providers. I don't think this is the case anymore, largely because you can duplicate virtual servers in the blink of an eye. In the old days, you could "ghost" a drive, which was a time-consuming process. Virtual machines have changed the game here, because redundancy is much easier—and much more affordable—to create and maintain than it used to be.

At my company, we have even outsourced our telephone service to the cloud using RingCentral. We have no landlines. The voice-over-IP

(VoIP) service is hosted in the cloud, as is our whole voice messaging system. If I need new phone lines, I simply add them online and buy the phones we want to hook up. No requirement for a service technician; no waiting to get it done. The only delay is how long it takes us to go to Best Buy—or the storage closet—and back to get more phones. We have more control and less cost, and the service is just as reliable as a landline would be.

Another consideration that is often left out of ROI analyses when considering cloud versus traditional computing is the fact that developers can activate these services without laying an extra burden on the IT department. This reduces internal operational and people costs within the IT department, and also can speed up deployment of important applications, negating the need to wait for availability of IT resources, or by making IT resources more effective.

It is also important to keep on top of the configurations and performance of your cloud computing provider. Do they keep their server base refreshed? You are paying by the hour, so you want to make sure you have access to high speeds. For some applications, it may be more cost effective to use an internal server. There is definitely a tipping point, though; when you have massive amounts of data or processing, it still makes more sense to put it in the cloud. For example, we do a great deal of personalization of content. This requires a lot of computing power and often access to large databases. We keep that in the cloud for those reasons. Also, if you have a third party vendor to maintain the software, it is easier to have them access it in the cloud than to give them access to your VPN.

Another good use of cloud computing is the ability to spin up new applications quickly and/or test them during development. We saw that from the Army and Pathwork Diagnostics examples cited earlier. Once the application is established, its physical location can be reevaluated.

In 2009, we did just that when we launched a new application, QReate& Track, a service that allows the easy generation, publishing and tracking of QR codes. More recently, we did the same thing with iFlyMobi, a tool for the easy creation of mobile-friendly websites. You can provision a virtual server and have it running in no time.

There are also significant advantages to remote hosting from an ongoing operational perspective. One weekend in the fall of 2007, our IT folks began seeing errors reported by our system, which was really a private cloud hosted at AT&T's data center. Most of our staff was unavailable that weekend, and we needed to get this resolved right away—and I have empowered my team to do that based on their good judgment, regardless of whether or not I am personally available. Adam Meixler, our primary IT engineer, contacted our data center, and they sent a technician to take a look. After about a half hour, they called us back with bad news—the server had failed to boot because it couldn't find the system drive. In this case the "system drive" was a RAID array of hard drives, and there were no failure lights on any of the individual drives. Adam worked with the on-site technician to troubleshoot, and they finally determined that the controller for the RAID array had failed. Adam was able to locate a vendor in Brooklyn who had the necessary parts, purchase them, and somehow convinced them to have one of their employeesemployee's couriercourier the controller to the data center. Then Adam had to clear the courier to enter the data center. The on-site technician performed a flawless replacement and had the machine back up and running by the end of the day. All of this without needing to get on a plane and see for himself!

When using a public cloud implementation, you are much less likely to experience this kind of thing because of the built-in redundancies. If you do, however, you really have no choice but to wait for it to come back up. This is something to consider in making the decision about exactly how you want to implement cloud computing.

Scaling Up/Scaling Down

The value of being able to rapidly scale down should not be underestimated either. Scaling up and down can be due to the need to address peak computing period. But it can also be due to an unexpected decline in business that requires a scale-down of IT resources. If you own those resources, you are basically stuck with them, or can sell them at a loss. But when using a cloud-based model, you can pull resources offline quickly and with little, if any, negative financial ramifications, assuming your contracts are structured appropriately.

In effect, operating in a public cloud allows you to activate services as needed, matching spending to the amount of profit that comes from this capability. It allows you to make sure you can tie your costs directly and precisely to whatever revenue comes through the door. If you have spikes in usage, ensure that those spikes are for the right reasons and with a cost curve that matches the corresponding revenue or business value that comes back to you as a result of that application scaling up. With a private cloud, even if it is hosted in a remote data center, you still have responsibility for providing and maintaining the hardware, although as in our story above, there are on-site resources that can help as part of the service agreement.

Like anything you outsource, you should ask yourself: Does this allow me to place more focus on my core business rather than the more mundane aspects of data center management—applying patches, software updates, adding servers, removing servers, installing client software…the list goes on. If the answer is yes, the cloud should be considered.

Cloud computing is not a panacea, though, and it may not always be cheaper than traditional models. It is important to have a clear understanding of all contractual terms and conditions. With traditional IT services, you tend to pay and account for these expenses on an annual basis. You should do the same calculations with the cloud model, and carefully weigh the benefits of a pay-as-you-go, self-serve model—remembering to account for all associated internal and external costs for both scenarios. Find out whether your service provider has off-peak pricing, and determine whether you can use those lower cost periods to run all or some of your applications. That's one way to keep costs in line.

Another approach is to look at your operations in layers or tiers. For example, you may have an Oracle database that does not scale or have much transiency. You may find it more cost effective to maintain that in house. Another tier might be application logic that doesn't scale much either. However, the third tier, the web tier, might be scaling up and down wildly. By hosting this tier in the cloud, and the other two internally, this hybrid model could save you significant dollars. Hosting all three tiers either in the cloud or traditionally might be extremely expensive. But by using the right platform for the right application set, you create the opportunity to save tremendous amounts of time and money.

By re-architecting applications to take full advantage of the cloud, or by building new applications you couldn't do before that leverage the cloud, you can scale down to the smallest possible computing footprint.

In thinking about the costs associated with traditional versus cloud computing, consider Starbucks, a classic when discussing and analyzing costs. When you buy that Grande Caramel Macchiato, which you might purchase several times a week, your cost is around the price of one drink. Mind you, we're not looking at the cost of you driving to that Starbucks, the time it takes for you to order and get your drink and so on. We're just looking at the cost of that tasty Starbucks drink. (And the benefit of all that caffeine may be more than worth that cost!) But when you add up the annual amount you spend, the result can be shocking. Starbucks would prefer that you only think about it one drink at a time—pay-as-you-go—because if you really thought about what you spend in an entire year with them, you would likely spill your coffee!

The same goes for rental cars. If you are in Chicago and need a car for a couple of days, it does not make sense to buy one, even though it costs less per hour to do so. Just as with cloud computing, you are paying for elasticity—the ability to add resources as the need gets bigger—or for a transient need where you only launch the application periodically, perhaps at the end of the quarter to close the books or to address other peak computing requirements.

Cloud-based services are not so different. It is a business decision you must make, weighing all of the pros and cons in your analysis. Also consider that once you are operating in the cloud, you must continue to periodically analyze your options; when and if it makes sense, operations can be moved to your own infrastructure.

Keep in mind that there may be "soft" values to cloud computing as well as hard dollar impact. Just like you get value from plunking down five bucks for that Grande Caramel Macchiato or taking advantage of rental car services, the ability to rapidly scale operations up and down may outweigh any added costs moving some of your computing to the cloud might incur.

Doing Business in the Digital Age

Faster time to market, lower costs, ability to quickly scale up or down, likely higher security and more ease of use—these are some of the benefits to cloud computing we have identified.

My own company, which was founded in the mid-1990s during the dot-com boom, and luckily is still in operation and doing well today, is a good example. I would estimate that about 30% of our computing takes place in the cloud. We deliver software as a service (more on that later) and were an early adopter of that model.

As a start-up, I don't know that we could have effectively hosted everything in-house. Of course, back then, the term cloud computing wasn't being used. Software as a service hadn't really been invented, and we were seeing the beginnings of what was called the Application Service Provider (ASP) model. It was more like outsourcing your physical data center, kind of a private cloud model of external hosting. It was a much more risky venture back then, for many reasons, not the least of which was the instability of the providers.

Our first Internet service provider was TEAC. Our connection to the outside world was a standard 56K telephone line and an analog modem. We had to keep pinging the server in an infinite loop or the phone line would shut down.

We then moved to data center outsourcer NaviSite. We were the second server to be installed in their facility, right next to Levi Strauss. Its biggest value proposition was the infrastructure, and security it provided. However, it was a peer-to-peer configuration or distributed architecture and did not have a direct pipe to the Internet, which is a basic feature of today's cloud computing providers. Exodus, our next stop, started out selling Internet backbone (access and bandwidth) before it got into data storage, so it had that advantage over NaviSite.

From there, it seemed like we were running from one data center to another as one after the other went belly-up—remember UUNet, MCIWorldCom, to name a couple? You figured these companies started this business model and would never go bankrupt. But they did, and left us, and many others, scrambling. When you are managing Fortune 100 data online, you cannot afford to be down!

We ultimately ended up using AT&T for hosting—and still do. They have been very good to us. When we migrated our external computing there, we had to do it with no down time. Our customers would not have tolerated down time, nor should they. That's a good part of why they use us instead of hosting internally. When moving everything to AT&T, we had to build a new configuration, and AT&T did that for us at no cost, including the use of loaner server capacity for 30 days at no charge. Believe me, they got their money's worth in the end, but we were very appreciative that they stuck their neck out for us in the beginning. Once we had our servers configured, they even had their technicians pack everything up, shipped it via a special shipping company, and had their network guys set everything up for us in their center.

In those days, we also had to sell our solution twice—once to the business line manager and next to IT. The latter was pretty resistant in the early days. The idea of hosting their data outside the firewall or giving an external application access inside their firewall was anathema. That has changed to some degree for most companies.

One reason we feel more comfortable with cloud-based computing is the stability of most of today's providers. Add to that the fact that, unlike early providers such as Exodus, these cloud computing sources are not relying on cloud computing revenues for their entire business. It is an added service, and probably for most, a relatively small part of their business. They will not go out of business based on the ups and downs of your peak and valley periods! (IBM, Amazon, Microsoft…)

The other consideration in today's dynamic business world is the compressed timeline of doing business. You can't necessarily give yourself weeks or months to get an application up and running. You may need it up in a few hours. An example would be an e-Commerce storefront. Suppose you are in the business of providing this storefront infrastructure, and a large retail client has an opportunity to add a specialty boutique storefront featuring new and unique products they have just contracted to retail.

It is September, and they need to have everything ready to go for the holiday season. They can't do it themselves in their own data center, so they turn to you. With your cloud-based, very scalable operation, you can have a prototype up and running in a few days, with testing complete and ready for launch well before Halloween. You are a hero and could very well make this retailer's holiday season even merrier than it might otherwise have been.

This success story will likely be followed by more business from this retailer—and from others as the word gets around.

Despite all the evidence that cloud computing brings businesses significant value—at least for some of its computing needs, a 2010 IBM survey of more than 1,500 CEOs worldwide revealed that close to 80% of them thought their environment would grow more complex in coming years, but fewer than half thought their companies were equipped to deal with this shift.

---

[15]Source: *What Every CEO Needs to Know about the Cloud*, By Andrew McAfee, Harvard Business Review, November 2011.

The survey team called it "the largest leadership challenge identified in eight years of research."[15] Wow.

Harvard Business Review's Andrew McAfee says, "The cloud is a topic CEOs must engage on, because many of the executives they typically delegate technology decisions to are precisely the wrong people to offer unbiased guidance. Most IT departments today are stretched thin with maintenance activities, leaving precious little bandwidth for development and new initiatives." Exactly the reason that cloud computing is attractive, allowing business units to, in many cases, bypass overburdened IT resources to be more nimble and responsive. But, oh , the politics of this. This is exactly why leadership at the top must be educated about the pros and cons of cloud computing—and mobile communications, too, by the way—so that the best interests of the organization can be pursued without politics or workload issues interfering.

McAfee argues that cloud computing is "a sea change—a deep and permanent shift in how computing power is generated and consumed. It's as inevitable and irreversible as the shift from steam to electric power in manufacturing, which was gaining momentum in America about a century ago. And just as that transition brought many benefits and opened up new possibilities to factory owners, so too will the cloud confer advantages on its adopters. At present, there's a lot of uncertainty and skepticism around the cloud, particularly among technology professionals who have deep expertise with, or attachment to, on-premise computing. Companies shouldn't give such people too much influence over plans to move into the cloud; that would be like putting the crew that ran the boiler and steam turbine in charge of electrifying a factory. The CEO and other senior business executives need to take responsibility for bringing their organizations into the era of cloud computing."

There is no question in my mind that McAfee is right on the money on this one. Well, it is a Harvard publication, after all, and McAfee is a principal research scientist at the Center for Digital Business in the

MIT Sloan School of Management—strong and credible credentials. But setting that aside … As you lead your company into the future, this is one area to which you, personally, should be paying attention. Don't miss the opportunities that cloud computing offers for making your company more nimble, streamlined and competitive. Those who have made the move have also found that while a certain set of anticipated benefits are assigned to this transition, once users get their hands on new, more up-to-date cloud-based applications, they are likely to surprise you with what they do with it. The unanticipated benefits can often outweigh the anticipated benefits, so true of most disruptive technologies.

Next, let's talk about Software as a Service (SaaS), and explore how this fits into the cloud computing world.

Software as a Service (SaaS): How Is It Different?

As one might intuit from the description of cloud computing, it is often delivering software as a service. This means that the software developer maintains one instance of the core software code, making it available to customers via the developer's servers or through a contractual arrangement with a provider of cloud computing resources. Each iteration of the software, as implemented by individual customers, can be customized to their particular needs, but the core software is basically the same for all users. Code is structured to make it easy for the developer to simultaneously upgrade all users as enhancements, new functionality and bug fixes are introduced into the core code, with minimal (if any) disruption to the user's operation. Most software-as-a-service contracts also include technical support, training, bug fixes, product enhancements and all major upgrades.

This is contrasted with the traditional licensed software model. With licensed software, the model likely most familiar to many companies, a software license is purchased and the software is installed on a server on the customer's corporate network, with the license fee paid up front. In this case, it is up to the user to maintain the server, add any necessary customizations (sometimes using professional services purchased from the software developer or third parties), and perhaps most importantly, perform upgrades as new versions become available. In many cases, the process of upgrading licensed software can be time-consuming and can require system downtime—an expensive undertaking when the software is core to business operations, such as an MIS or ERP solution. Remember, it is not just upgrading the software on the server itself, but many times it also requires upgrades to all of the workstations in the enterprise that are using this software package.

In addition, new releases can deliver unexpected results due to feature changes, software bugs and other implementation issues. In a worst case scenario, users may have to go back to the previous software version while these issues are being resolved. For this reason, users may postpone software upgrades or forego them altogether, often missing out on advances that could be beneficial to their businesses. In addition, developers of licensed software typically accumulate a number of fixes, features and functions into a new release, offering these releases on a periodic basis, perhaps annually, semi-annually or quarterly. This accumulation of changes to the code also increases the possibility that an upgrade will have unexpected results and makes it harder to narrow down the cause.

One way to explain the difference between the two is to think of them as software as a service, versus software as a *product*.

The software-as-a-service model is different from licensed software in that upgrades can be made more frequently, even on a daily or hourly basis, without disruption to operations, and without multiple changes that make it more difficult to track down the source of issues that might arise after an upgrade occurs. Most SaaS solutions are offered on a month-to-month subscription basis. This induces the software developer to provide frequent updates as well as benchmark customer service in order to retain customers. In a licensed software model, the developer has the money up front (license fee) and may be less incented to address issues rapidly, preferring to wait for an appropriate accumulation of changes to incorporate in a new release. SaaS users also have a choice as to whether or not they turn on updates as they become available and can pick and choose which changes to turn on.

This model allows users to be selective. Oftentimes with licensed software, when an update arrives, it is an all-or-nothing proposition. And then you have to wait for the next upgrade—next month, next quarter, next year—to get fixes to problems that might have been precipitated by the last upgrade (although if it is a big enough problem, most software providers will provide patches that correct the problem pending the next release—and installing them is another consumer of IT time).

Finally, SaaS solutions generally offer a lower up-front investment. This likely includes a moderate set-up fee and a pay-as-you-go monthly subscription or pay-per-transaction model. This financial model typically also includes customer support and all upgrades, and does not require users to trouble themselves with performing the updates. Because the software is hosted in the cloud, it is accessible from any computing device with a browser. This means it is cross-platform and not necessarily reliant on a specific version of the user's computer operating system. A good SaaS solution will also comply with industry standards. The advantage here is that it is easier and less costly for a user to change mid-stream if the service is not meeting requirements. Data can be extracted and exported to a new solution that also complies with these standards without the costly and error-prone need to rekey or recreate data. Many licensed software packages use proprietary database structures that can make data extraction difficult.

Companies may be reluctant to explore the SaaS model, resisting the concept of monthly payments for software that the company never owns. However, this concept is not much different than leasing a vehicle or a press. Besides, legally you don't own licensed software either; you only license its use. The market is growing more accustomed to the SaaS model as is evidenced by the success of such SaaS solutions as Salesforce.com. Salesforce.com is an especially relevant example, since the solution maintains sensitive customer

relationship management (CRM) data in the cloud, and its many users are benefiting from the ease of use and deployment, as well as the scalability of this particular solution.

One final important point: Cloud computing and SaaS are related but not identical. There is a delineation between pure SaaS and cloud computing in that a SaaS solution can be hosted in the cloud, but it can also be delivered in a self-host model. In this instance, typically deployed by larger organizations, the software and data reside on an internal server or servers which the enterprise must maintain. However, software updates are still delivered automatically via the Internet, relieving the enterprise IT staff of that task and ensuring that the software stays current. The self-hosted SaaS model operates as a virtual cloud within the enterprise firewall. The enterprise is responsible for scaling the installation as transaction and data volumes exceed existing server capacity, a responsibility of the software service provider in a true cloud-based model.

Another benefit of SaaS that should not be underestimated is the ease of use. Most users are familiar with the web and this familiarity can ease the learning curve for new browser-based SaaS applications.

Next up is mobile computing and the effect that smartphones, tablets and other totally untethered computing is having on everything from shopping habits to marketing, gaming, information distribution and more. We will talk about what is happening in the mobile marketplace and how you should be thinking about your untethered business in light of these developments.

Chapter Three: The Magic of Mobile

We live in a mobile culture. Regardless of whether your customers are businesses or consumers, they are more likely to be in the car, in a restaurant, or out and about than they are at home or in the office. Mobile phones have become the *de facto* method of communication.

In fact, according to research firm MobiThinking in 2011, there are 5.3 billion mobile subscribers worldwide; that's 77% of the world's population! In the U.S., 25% of Internet users are mobile only. Tablets such as the Apple iPad, Samsung Galaxy Tab and Kindle Fire are another form of mobile computing that is growing exponentially. In fact, Cisco Systems projects that between 2010 and 2015, mobile data use is expected to grow by a factor of 26with a compound annual growth rate (CAGR) of 92%—and no, those aren't typos. See the chart below.

Figure 2. Mobile Data Traffic per Mobile Connection: 2009, 2010, 2015

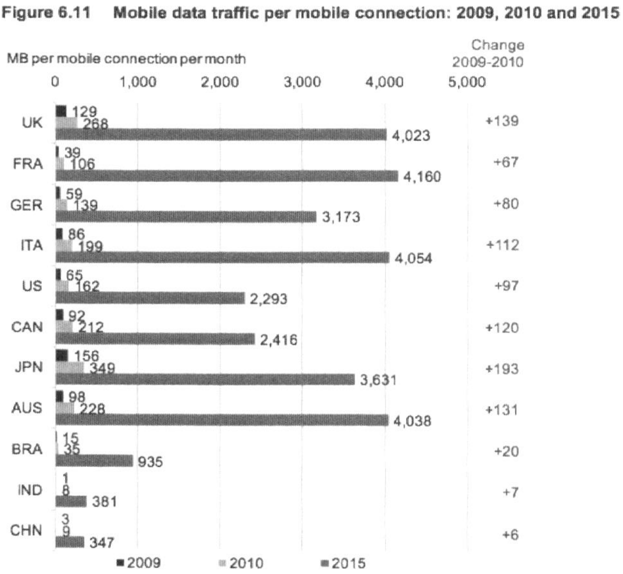

Figure 2.Cisco Systems' Visual Networking Index June 1, 2011, via PaidContent.org

We will address both smartphones and tablets in this chapter and discuss how they affect the customer communications arena.

The Internet in Our Pockets: The Balance of Power Has Shifted

The Internet changed the balance of power between businesses and consumers. Consumers now have instantaneous access to a wealth of information, and they are increasingly choosing when, where and how to receive that information—or even whether to receive it at all. Now, with the Internet literally in our pockets, the balance of power is shifting even further.

An example of how this power shift is playing out can be seen in the response of retailer Best Buy to the growing trend of consumers coming into the store, finding the product they want, and then comparing prices online from their phones. Initially, Best Buy began removing bar codes from product displays. This made it a bit more difficult—though not impossible—for customers to quickly compare prices and choose to buy from Best Buy or not. As the 2011 holiday buying season approached, Best Buy seemed to give in to the inevitable, with an advertising campaign that promised they would match any price, at the time of sale, or even afterward. This is a huge business strategy shift that is completely driven by the change in consumer behavior and the balance of power shift. If it works, it should help Best Buy retain in-store sales, but it is not clear what the profit impact will be long term. However, the company apparently also removed free WiFi access from its stores! It remains to be seen how consumers react to that very strange move.

Target is another retailer that is trying to discourage the in-store price comparison trend. According to a *Wall Street Journal* article, the company sent a letter to its vendors in early January 2012 asking them to provide either exclusive merchandise or lower prices and may be considering offering a subscription service that would offer customers lower prices on frequently purchased items. This seems to be a more customer-focused approach than Best Buy's response to this trend.

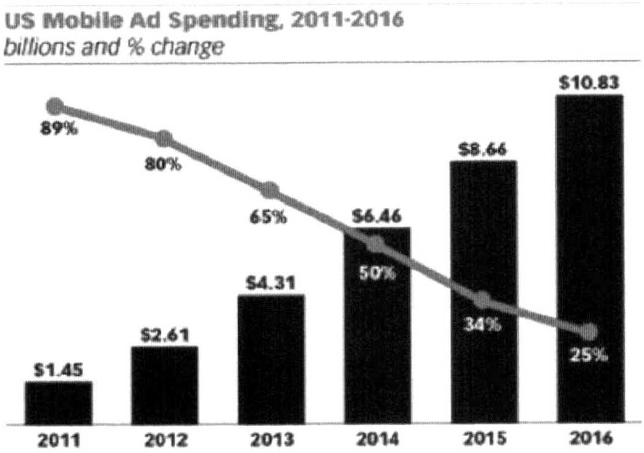

According to the 2011 Mobile Internet Attitudes Report from Antenna Software, one in five U. S. mobile phone owners uses the mobile Internet every day. On Device Research reports that 25% of U. S. mobile phone users are *mobile only*. In other words, they do not (or very rarely) use a desktop, laptop, or tablet to access the Web. They are truly untethered. In October of 2011, for the first time, according to CTIA, a cellular industry trade group, there were more wireless subscriber connections than people, mostly because of business accounts and people with multiple cell phones.[16]

Smart marketers are taking it mobile.

Why Mobile Marketing

Mobile is the future of marketing. Mobile affects every aspect of your customers' lives. Users are rapidly migrating from feature phones to smartphones. In fact, in 2011, smartphones represented 63% of mobile phones in the U.S., 51% in Europe, 19% in the Asia-Pacific, 18% in Africa/Middle East, and 17% in Latin America.[17] This means

[16] *Wireless Devices now Outnumber U.S. Population*, by Mike Freeman, Sign On San Diego, October 11, 2011

[17] *The Elusive Long Tail of Mobile Shipments*, by Matos Kapetanakis, Vision Mobile, November 2, 2011

Image Source: emarketer.com

an increasing number of mobile phones have bigger screens, more graphic capabilities, more and faster connectivity and more computing power.

Already, there are many people who live their entire business and personal lives on their phones. From coupon clipping to product research to social media, there's an app for that. Mobile marketing gives marketers near immediate access to these savvy untethered individuals — no matter where they are or what they are doing.

There are many ways to reach the untethered mobile customer:

- Text Messages
- Email
- Mobile Search
- Mobile Websites
- Mobile Video
- QR Codes
- Social Media

Let's look at some of the ways your business can take advantage of untethered marketing opportunities in a mobile world.

Text Messaging

Texting has become a way of life. The average American mobile phone user now sends more texts per month than they make phone calls (hopefully not while driving!).

ABI Research estimated that consumers worldwide would send more than 7 trillion (yes, trillion) SMS messages in 2011. Of all the SMS messages sent on a daily basis, 98% are opened, with 83% opened within 3 minutes.[18]

---

[18] *Is SMS Marketing Still a Viable Strategy?*, by James Bentham, posted to Techipedia, December 20, 2011.

For many users, especially younger folks, texting is preferred to phone calls; I personally find that texting is the best way to contact my sons. They don't always answer the phone, and they don't listen to voice mail. We rarely even answer the landline at our house; it's mostly used by telemarketers. In fact, I keep wondering why we even have it. Texting my sons, gets their attention right away. Keep in mind that my sons, ages 16, 18 and 26, represent your target market of the future. In fact, Nielsen reported that U.S. teens tripled their mobile data consumption in 2011, with teens between the age of 13 and 17 consuming an average of 320 megabytes of mobile data per month and averaging 3,417 SMS and MMS messages per month during the third quarter of the year. But for a growing number of older consumers, that future is now and texting can be a valuable and viable component of your marketing plan as long as it is relevant and not perceived as being too invasive.

There are a variety of ways to integrate text messaging into your marketing mix:

- Broadcast text messages
- Invite people to text back short codes ("text BOGOFREE to 12345")[19]
- Use triggered text alerts based on time or location

The Hilton Hotel Group, for example, is using texts to alert guests about on-site specials and promotions right on their mobile phones. By getting the messages out to the right people at exactly the right time, the company has boosted offer redemptions by 10% to 25%.

When Dunkin' Donuts wanted to market hot lattes to high school and college age students in the Boston area, it used a combination of radio advertising and mobile Internet (WAP) ads[20] — "text in to DD-123" — to drive in-store redemption of mobile coupons. The result? A 21% increase in store traffic and redemption of the mobile coupon.

---

[19]BOGO = Buy One Get One in "text talk"

[20]The Mobile Marketing Association (www.mmaglobal.com) has defined mobile web banner (WAP) specifications. WAP stands for Wireless Application Protocol, a protocol developed to allow efficient transmission of optimized Internet content to wireless phones.

Winn-Dixie, a supermarket chain headquartered in Jacksonville, Florida, is using an SMS program that allows consumers to opt in to automatically have prescriptions refilled. Once a user agrees to participate in the program, Winn-Dixie's pharmacy automatically keeps tabs on medications and will remind consumers when it is time to get a refill.

Walgreens has a similar program. The company is heavily advertising its iPhone app, which is also available for Android. The Walgreens mobile banner ad reads, "Refill prescriptions in seconds," with an image of the Walgreens logo. When users tap the ad, they are taken to an in-app landing page where they can download the app from inside the ad, keeping consumers interacting with the branded environment and the marketing message. The app allows users to scan the bar code on their prescriptions to automatically reorder or find the nearest Walgreens location. At the time of this writing, Walgreens was reporting that 25% of online prescriptions were refilled via mobile. In addition to the convenience for the consumer, Walgreens can capture usage data that allows the company to increasingly tailor communications with individuals with coupons, promotions and other personalized promotions.

Business use of text messaging will only continue to grow. Juniper research projects that by 2016, application-to-person (A2P) messaging will overtake person-to-person (texting) messaging, and be worth more than $70 billion. A2P examples include automated alerts from banks offers from retailers and m-tickets.

Short Codes and Coupons

You can also use mobile for "pull" marketing by allowing consumers to download coupons from other sources, including blogs, e-newsletters, and websites. Or, as in the Dunkin' Donuts example, they can be encouraged to text short codes to receive special offers.

For the past seven years, Clear Channel Broadcasting has been enabling radio stations to interact with listeners on a real-time basis via text messaging short codes. When listeners send a text to short code 97373, they receive an invitation from the radio station to join the Mobile Click Club. Stations use keywords as triggers for listeners to receive information they want. For example, text 'Now Playing' to the short code 97373 to receive a message back about the song they are currently listening to.

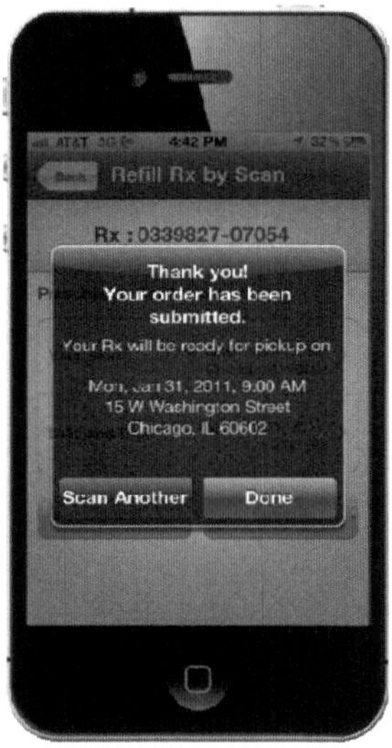

In another example, the manufacturer of Starburst candy wanted to engage teens by getting them to text a promotional short code found in specially marked packs of Starburst Fruit Chews. Teens could text the code J-U-I-C-Y (58429) using any cell phone carrier, and online at starburst.com, to find out instantly via a return message if they've won "juiced-up" technology prizes like a 42-inch flat-screen TV, an iPod Photo, and more. Starburst reported that daily online visits nearly doubled during the promotional period. Text messaging accounted for 40% more traffic than anticipated. Text marketing produces results!

Kohl's Department Stores is also investing in mobile tools to make shopping easier. In the example shown here, Kohl's hopes consumers will subscribe to its text messaging program to convey offers for Kohls.com purchases by receiving five messages per month. Recipients can purchase items right from the phone offer, anywhere they happen to be. Specifying the number of messages to expect up-front is a smart move. Five messages a month doesn't sound like that much, and may encourage customers who otherwise wouldn't subscribe, not wanting to be inundated by marketing messages.

Another great story comes from Alon Brands. The company owns 300 7-Eleven stores in the Southwestern U.S. and sells gasoline to another 600 convenience stores. The company was looking for a way to build an opt-in database that would enable it to conduct future marketing efforts more efficiently and lay the groundwork for a loyalty program. The instant win free gas promotion integrated radio, billboard, point-of-sale, Web, social, mobile, email and database marketing. In the first month, 9,000 customers signed up via mobile. Over a two month period, more than 25,000 customers signed up via mobile, Facebook and the Web. More than 50% of those who signed up provided multiple pieces of personal information about themselves and 30% provided a full profile. For the promotion, radio and point-of-sale ads encouraged consumers to text the word GAS to a mobile phone short-code and this automatically registered them for the free fuel sweepstakes. By any measure, this campaign was a huge success.

Triggered Texts

You can also send triggered texts based on timing or geographic location. For example:

- As mentioned earlier, Winn-Dixie and Walgreens are now offering prescription text alerts to notify customers when their prescriptions are ready and to make it easier for them to refill prescriptions by reminding them when the refill is due.
- A growing number of restaurants use text messages to replace traditional buzzers for patrons waiting for a table.
- Doctors and other appointment-based businesses send SMS reminders to patients reminding them about their appointments that day to reduce no-shows and last-minute cancellations.
- An important element of many cross-media campaigns is a triggered notification to sales reps when a prospect has responded to a campaign call to action. By sending these alerts to sales reps

via SMS, sales reps may be able to take quick action to ensure conversion to a sale.

- Southwest Airlines, in response to a horrific 2008 hurricane season, started building out a proactive service approach via mobile. By the end of 2009, Southwest had sent more than 5.7 million messages with an error rate of less than 10 percent. While these were customer service messages related to flight cancellations and delays, the success of the new communications process bodes well for the use of this medium for relevant marketing messages as well. As for Southwest, the company reported that its bill was cut in half by using this automated means of notification rather than outbound calling from its call center.

You can trigger by location, too. Imagine being able to deliver a coupon alert at the very moment your customer is walking by the store!

Mobile Messaging Mechanics

Mobile marketing of this type sounds complicated, but it's not. Integrated marketing software solutions, like ilinkONE Version 8 from my company, make it easy to send text messages to people in your contact database. Simply search for contacts via a wide variety of filter criteria, and then click "send SMS."

For example, you could pull up a list of people that have opted-in to receive SMS messages from you. With this type of software, you can craft the message you would like to send and have it reach the proper target audience. It is easy and direct.

Mobile and Social Media

Another way to take advantage of mobile is through social media. Social networking activity — one of today's fastest growing marketing channels —is huge on mobile devices. Chapter Six contains lots more information on this topic.

According to comScore, Inc., 72.2 million Americans accessed social networking sites or blogs on their mobile devices in August 2011, an increase of 37 percent over the prior year.[21]

"Social media is one of the most popular and fastest growing mobile activities, reaching nearly one third of all U.S. mobile users," said Mark Donovan, comScore senior vice president for mobile. "This behavior is even more prevalent among smartphone owners with three in five accessing social media each month, highlighting the importance of apps and the enhanced functionality of smartphones to social media usage on mobile devices."

Mobile access to Facebook grew 50% between August 2010 and August 2011, while Twitter and LinkedIn access grew 75% and 69% respectively, over the same period.

As smartphone usage grows, social media on mobile will explode. Understanding how mobile users interact with social media is important for brands looking to engage with on-the-go consumers.

The comScore study reflected that mobile social networkers were also likely to interact with brands on these sites with more than half (52.9 percent) reading posts from organizations/brands/events. One in three mobile social networkers received a coupon/offer/deal, with one in four (27.7 percent) clicking on an ad while on a social networking site. This opens up significant opportunities for marketers to increase the relevance of their engagement with consumers by using location-based

---

[21]Social Networking On-The-Go: U.S. Mobile Social Media Audience Grows 37 Percent in the Past Year, comScore, October 20, 2011

services. (There is a whole section on location based services (LBS) in this chapter).

What does this mean for you? If you are doing social media marketing, you must have a mobile-optimized site. As consumers click through links and share information, they will be coming to your site. When they do, you need to provide them with a mobile-optimized experience in order to engage them and keep them coming back.

Mobile Marketing: Where Does It Fit

While mobile marketing is the hot new medium, for most companies, it clearly won't be the only medium used to communicate with customers and prospects. Even in an untethered enterprise, there is a need for "tethered" marketing as well. So where does mobile marketing fit?

Just like television didn't totally obsolete radio and print, neither does mobile marketing obviate the need to use more conventional means of marketing.

For most businesses, it is another medium—albeit an important one—to add to the mix. The HSN example is a good one that links mobile to broadcast. Using QR or other barcodes and mobile-readable symbols is one way to both make print (and broadcast) interactive and to easily integrate mobile into the mix. The key challenge for your business is to segment your markets to enable better targeting of communications, whether to customers or prospects, and use the medium or media that are most appropriate *at the time*. In other words, use the right medium to target the right audience at the right time. For most recipients of your communications, the preferred medium is quite fluid, and it is important to understand what that is, often to an individual level.

Custom XM, based in Little Rock, Arkansas, is a marketing services provider that successfully transitioned from a traditional printer.

President of Custom XM, Paul Strack, has said that the transition's success has been attributed in large part to, "embracing new technology, cross media, PURLs, QR codes, augmented reality, and the mobile environment."

Regarding mobile, Paul says that it is "another arrow in our quiver, just like QR codes or text messaging. Print used to be the dominant answer, and now that's not the case. When we talk to clients to make marketing more effective, if mobile fits, that's what we recommend. "

Paul noted that over recent years, Custom XM's most successful marketing efforts have been quarterly lunch and learns. They reach out to clients and prospects, as well as the local chamber of commerce, and promote it across all channels. Then, they develop a mobile site that has the contents of the seminar on it, as well as the name of the presenter, and all other relevant details about the event.

"We integrate a PURL campaign, create mobile landing pages, and because of that," Paul says, "we have had great success."

Michael Smith, VP of Tourism for Jones Media, spoke about many of his clients embracing mobile marketing and seeing "exponential results."

"The key is to keep information short and provide a valuable offer to the end user," Smith said. "Keep in mind destination tourism markets are unique in how they use the auto-responder for tourist and subscription based campaigns for locals."

The bottom line is that the most effective communications program is one that combines multiple touches and multiple media in an integrated, relevant and measurable way. Mobile is one of the media you should be considering in that mix. We'll have more detail about exactly how to do that in Chapter Seven.

Optimizing for Mobile

So what does optimizing for mobile mean? It means that while you may not need to do anything differently in your social media marketing, you do need a mobile-optimized website. When web content is accessed by a mobile device, it isn't just putting the same content on a different device. Mobile phones have smaller screens. They have different formatting requirements. And there is a huge array of configurations from manufacturer to manufacturer, model to model. As one example, handset maker Nokia has over 3,000 different formats in its phone portfolio. To give people a positive experience, information must be organized and presented differently depending on the target device.

Not too long ago, I was presenting at a mobile marketing event. I asked folks how long many of them had a mobile-optimized corporate site. While several indicated they had a mobile-optimized site, a deeper dive into the conversation revealed that many just adjusted for screen resolution. While this is better than nothing, it is not the way to go.

Part of the problem companies have in moving to a mobile-friendly or mobile-first strategy is leaving it in the hands of IT. I love the IT guys, don't get me wrong. Whatever would we do without them? But decisions about how to optimize your website for mobile—what should be presented and how—should be a marketing, not an IT, decision. Marketing should guide the IT department in this type of deployment. This is a strategic marketing decision. Your website is a marketing tool, not an IT tool. In many companies, IT owns the website and is responsible for making all of the changes. This is a legacy behavior from the early days that desperately needs to be abandoned. There are a wide variety of tools available that allow people who are not particularly IT savvy, or who don't know HTML coding, to make changes to the site themselves.

Marketing can and should own the content and should be able to respond very quickly to dynamically changing market conditions. Solutions such as Drupal, an open source content management solution (CMS); WordPress, which has evolved way beyond its roots as free blogging software; and Joomla have completely changed the game, placing capability in the hands of marketers that allows them to own web content, as they should.

In terms of mobile optimization, the bar is continually being raised. In the early days of mobile, users were excited to be able to access the web from their phones and were much less critical about the quality of the experience. Those days are over, and expectations are much higher now.

In a recent interview of Strangeloop president Josh Bixby, O'Reilly Radar writer Mac Slocum said, "Now, most customers expect a full and fast web experience whether they're on a desktop, tablet or phone. The companies that offer that are poised to succeed. And for those that don't, ridicule will be the least of their concerns."[22] Bixby says that it is a mistake to think of the web and the mobile web as two different things, saying, "Using these terms is helpful for discussing differences in how people browse via different devices, but at the end of the day, it's all one web. Users want the same breadth and depth of content, no matter what device they're using."

Mobile and Social Media

He also points out that an increasing amount of mobile traffic is coming from tablets, which have an even different set of formatting requirements. (More on tablets later in this chapter.)

One way to evaluate the effectiveness of your mobile website is to compare statistics for mobile versus desktop visitors. The numbers should be commensurate. If you are getting an average of 6.3 page views per visitor from the desktop but only 2.3 from mobile, that may indicate that the mobile interface needs an overhaul.

Platform Choices

Especially in the U.S., Apple receives a great deal of recognition for its mobile platforms. This leads some developers to focus on the Apple platform exclusively. By doing this, however, they may be missing the boat. Before media hype lulls you into focusing your marketing/ development budget on the Apple platform exclusively, consider this: 96.5 percent of global mobile users don't have one – mostly they use Nokia or Samsung; and even among smartphone users 84 percent don't have an Apple, according to MobiThinking 2011 data. In April of 2011, research firm Gartner predicted that 468 million smartphones would be sold in 2011, a 57.7% increase over 2010. Of those phones, 38.5 percent were expected be powered by the Android operating system. As 2011 closed out, however, those projections

---

[22] *You can't get away with a bad mobile experience anymore,* an interview with Joshua Bixby, President, Strangeloop, by Mac Slocum, December 14, 2011

proved to be understated. Millennial Media reported in October of 2011 that Android had a whopping 56% market share, compared to Apple's 28%.By 2015, Gartner expected that 631 million smartphones would be sold, approaching half of those Android. Those numbers are obviously pretty fluid and could change significantly by 2015. Check out our operating system section later in this chapter for more information about the various platforms, their market share and their outlook.

Mobile Web Sites versus Mobile Apps

In Chapter Four, we will go into greater detail about mobile apps. But for now, suffice it to say that mobile app is shorthand for mobile application, a term used to describe Internet applications that run on smartphones, tablets and other mobile devices. A mobile-friendly or mobile-optimized web site is accessed from a phone or tablet using a browser, such as Safari, Firefox, Chrome or Internet Explorer. An app, on the other hand, is a software application that is launched from the device. Both approaches are important to pursue in a mobile world. See Chapter Four for more details on this important topic, and lots of examples of how companies are leveraging mobile apps to drive both visibility and revenues.

Are You Making a Terrible Impression?

You might think your traditional website is just fine, but as mobile marketing guru Jeremy Epstein has written, "Here's a newsflash: if you have a Web site, you're already in the mobile world — and the chances are you're making a terrible impression."

How do you make the kind of impression that dazzles rather than disappoints? I recommend the following:

- Create a mobile-optimized version of your website.
- Optimize text, images, and widgets for mobile.
- Provide key points in sound bites/ short stories appropriate to a mobile audience.

- Select your content with a mobile audience in mind.
- Add logic to your main website to automatically direct people to the mobile version when they view your content on their phone.
- Test, test, test.

Sales Pitch Alert: One easy way to get into mobile websites is by using iFlyMobi.com, which allows you to take your existing content and quickly cut and paste to create a new, easy-to-use mobile site. Using this inexpensive solution, you can have a mobile site in less than an hour!

There are other solutions out there, of course. Whatever you choose, make sure that it incorporates device-sensing technology. That is, the software should be able to determine the exact device that is being used to access and deliver the content in the appropriate format. Content delivered to a Blackberry screen that is formatted for an iPhone will not do a good job of representing you or your brand.

Another option is to develop applications for mobile, or apps. In Chapter Four we will go into this option in greater detail. Basically, an app can be downloaded by the mobile user to make it easier to interact with the brand. For example, American Airlines offers an app that lets users check flight schedules, create a digital boarding pass that eliminates the need for a paper boarding pass, check mileage or upgrade status, and manage their account with the airline. Conference calling service FreeConference.com offers a free app that allows users to schedule and manage conference calls right from their smartphone.

When thinking about apps and the mobile web for your business, there are some things to consider. An app is built for the particular smartphone or tablet you have. Since most smartphones have their own operating system, applications need to be specifically designed for each.

The mobile web is characterized by the interfaces that run on the Internet. As wireless speeds continue to mature, the mobile web will only continue to improve in efficiency. But how do you decide between an app and a mobile website?

MobiThinking reports that U.S. consumers prefer mobile browsers for banking, travel, shopping, local info, news, video, sports and blogs. They prefer apps for games, social media, maps and music. More fuel to the fire for a mobile-optimized web site for your business … but keep in mind that a well-thought-out business app can make interacting with your brand even easier than using a mobile-optimized web site.

More than 300,000 mobile apps were developed in the three years beginning with 2009. Apple has seen more than 25 billion app downloads and Android has seen more than 10 million.[23]

Although one in four apps that are downloaded are never used again, your app can be different if it is relevant, easy to use and delivers a unique value, such as the convenience of scheduling a conference call from your phone, or having your boarding pass displayed digitally on a smartphone.

Mobile Video

Don't forget about video as a marketing tool. According to Google, YouTube alone accounts for 200 million mobile video playbacks every day. And video is an increasingly important component of marketing efforts, both on the web and for mobile. There is even a marketing council dedicated to this topic! The Web Video Marketing Council (www.webvideomarketing.org) has lots of resources for staying in touch with emerging trends, case studies, white papers, web video news and more.

YouTube is the #2 search engine, if you are not using it you are reducing your chances of being found on the Internet.

---

[23] Apple Ahead Of Google With 25B App Downloads, informationweek.com, March 5, 2012

One of the newest options for video is the ability to personalize video messages, much as we have personalized printed and email communications for some time. Philadelphia-based TGI created a cross-media campaign to attract customers through a personalized video. QR codes that direct to a specialized video add a personal touch – and add an air of originality Marketers can take advantage of tools the way TGI didto spiff up their marketing efforts and drive higher response rates.

Interactive audiovisual content is more engaging, interactive and responsive than static communications. And regardless of the medium, to the extent you can make communications, including video, more relevant, whether it is by personalizing messages or gearing them toward specific target audiences, the data doesn't lie: This stuff works!

Video, and particularly business-oriented video, is a growth area. According to Interactive Media Strategies,[24] overall spending on online business video technologies is expected to grow to more than $2 billion annually by 2015. The firm has been formally measuring and forecasting market spending patterns since 2006.

According to recent reports from both eMarketer and Gartner, mobile video ads are poised for the fastest growth of all the mobile ad platforms in the U.S. through 2015. In fact, mobile video ads will generate more revenue in 2015 than banners and rich media generated in 2011, according to eMarketer.[25] This growth could be hampered by data plans—consumers won't want marketing messages to eat up their entire data plan, that's for sure. In some countries, incoming messages are free. If U.S. carriers could get their arms around that one, the entire scenario could change dramatically. Fat chance, though, in my humble opinion.

---

[24]*Business Video Market Forecast, 2011-2015*, by Steve VonderHaar, Research Director, Interactive Media Strategies

[25]*3 new ad units you can't ignore*, by NickhilJakatdar, iMedia Connection, December 16, 2011, published by the Web Video Marketing Council.

Some of the elements most likely to be seen in mobile video ads include:

- Click to purchase product placement that allows users to purchase any product shown in the video with one click.
- Click to video, where they user can choose to launch the video by clicking on a banner ad.
- Video alert, allowing subscribers to be notified when a new video—from any source—is available.

According to Yahoo, ad recall by people who viewed a mobile ad was 15 percent higher than any other channel, and InsightExpress found that mobile video ads create twice as much ad awareness as online video campaigns.[26]

CustomXM had a creative use for mobile video promotion. They placed a QR Code on a printed ad that pointed to a YouTube video upon scanning. This video introduced the audience to a sales rep, essentially forging a meaningful relationship. Scan the QR Code to view the creative video that Custom XM did for this ad.

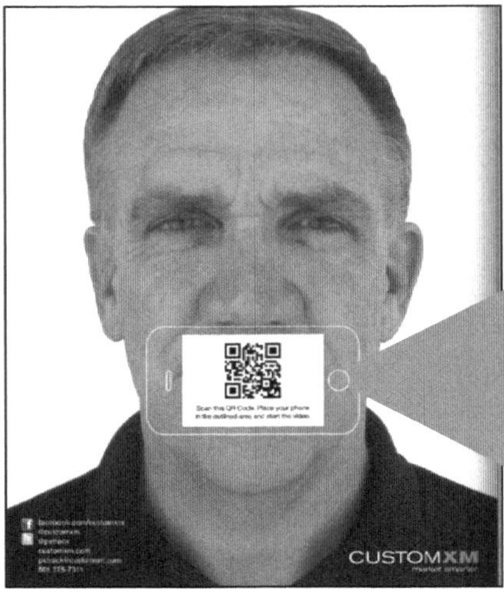

[26] 5 *best-practice tips for designing a mobile video campaign*, by UjjalKohli, published in Mobile Marketer, July 11, 2011.

UjjalKohli, CEO of Rhythm NewMedia, offered these five best-practice tips for designing a mobile video campaign:

- Run multiple types of video ads to reach the largest possible audience
- Combine video and display advertising to increase engagement
- A tap-to-interactive video option can create a very immersive brand experience with long-form video ads
- Custom buttons create a unique, interactive brand experience in video ads; include such things as tap to web site, tap to share on Facebook, tap to add to calendar or tap to buy from <name the store>
- Branding is most effective when ads are displayed alongside premium content

Beyond advertising, video also plays a growing role in mobile direct marketing, whether these videos are served up directly to mobile devices or incorporated into mobile-optimized landing pages.

Mobile Search

In the world of mobile marketing, you also need to pay attention to mobile search. Consumers are actively searching for products and services on their mobile phones—that means they are looking for you.

In fact, a recent study (and one of my favorites!) conducted by InsightExpress[27] found that when it comes to finding information to compare brands and products while in the store, 67% of men and 54% of women said they would reach for their mobile phone before asking a salesperson for help. Sixty-six percent of men and 59% of women would check reviews, and 53% and 38%, respectively, would check prices at other locations.

[27] *Mobile Consumer Research: 3Q 2011 Digital Consumer Portrait* (1,300 U.S. consumers participated in this online survey)

In a development not likely to please retailers, and another example of how much control consumers have these days, *The New York Times* reported that an array of mobile-only deals were lined up for Black Friday 2011 to pick off shoppers as they stood in crowded checkout lines. This includes offers from purveyors such as the Gilt Groupe, Amazon and HSN.

Efficient Frontier reports that 10% to 15% of search traffic, on average, comes from mobile devices. In specific markets, these numbers can double. Additionally, Efficient Frontier reports that 5.4% of all paid search impressions come from mobile devices. By the end of 2011, it is expected that between 7% and9.5% of search advertising dollars will be spent on mobile.

According to Jonathan Rosenberg, SVP at Google, in October of 2010,[28] mobile delivered an annualized run rate of over US$1billion in revenues to Google.

He said, "This means that the people accessing our products and services through their mobile phones are adding a billion dollars annually to our existing revenue streams. Wow. Clearly this is the future of search on the Internet. More people in more countries are coming online from smartphones. Our mobile search queries have grown five times over the last couple of years." With the addition of mobile app Google Shopper, this number is only likely to grow. More detail about Google Shopper and other search-related apps is provided in Chapter Four.

---

[28]Via MobiThinking.com, December 2011

Once again, this increases the urgency of having a mobile-optimized website in place. When mobile users click through to your site, it must be easy to navigate and easy for them to make an inquiry, make a purchase, or take some other action. This is particularly important in verticals like restaurants automotive, consumer electronics, finance and insurance, and beauty and personal care, which hold the highest share of mobile searches.

Mobile Purchases/Payments

Not only are people searching on mobile phones, but they are making buying decisions and purchasing using their mobile phone, as well as using these devices for other types of mobile payments. According to the Aite Group, U.S. mobile bill payments will reach $214 billion in 2015, up from $16 billion in 2010. In the 2011 holiday season, mobile purchases skyrocketed. On Thanksgiving Day, online sales rose 39% over the previous year, and 15.2% of online traffic came from mobile devices (up from 6.45% the previous year).[29] More importantly, mobile shoppers typically spent more than desktop shoppers - all the more reason to place immediate focus on delivering an exceptional mobile shopping experience.

This even includes luxury items. According to a report in Online Media Daily, more than one-quarter of iPhone, iPod touch, and Android users plan to buy a car in the next year. They may not be buying it through their phones, but nearly eight in 10 (78%) will use their mobile device as part of the process.

Digital marketing software company Kenshoo reported that in the 2011 holiday season, personal computers still accounted for the lion's share of both clicks and revenues (86% and 92% respectively) for online shopping driven by search. Tablets delivered the highest average order size and 7% of all revenue driven by paid search advertising, and the company's study seemed to indicate that mobile phones were primarily used for quick searches, locating products or stores, or placing phone call inquiries as opposed to completing actual transactions.[30]

---

[29]Source: IBM Benchmark monitoring service, comScore

[30]*2011 U.S. Online Retail Holiday Shopping Report*,Kenshoo, January 10, 2012

Fandango, a division of Comcast, sells tickets to more than 16,000 screens and is another beneficiary of this growing trend. The recent release of Twilight: Breaking Dawnsaw 22% of its tickets sold via mobile devices, breaking a Fandango record that was previously held by the last Harry Potter movie that opened in July of 2011 (20%). Buying tickets this way also gives Fandango and its partners ways to gather data on ticket-purchasing habits that could help them better target likely movie-goers with relevant offers or ads.

Big box retailer Home Depot was the first to jump in with a PayPal-enabled mobile payment solution at some of its stores. This was the first—and likely not the last (PayPal was reportedly working with 20+ retailers at the time of this writing)—retailer to sign up to PayPal's strategy of bridging online and in-store traffic for retailers. PayPal's mobile wallet solution, along with others such as Google Wallet, are gaining traction more slowly than expected, but are certainly a sign of what is to come in the future. Perhaps it will take wider adoption of near-field communications (NFC) to get them to really take hold.

Nevertheless, if you want to sell more, it is important to incorporate mobile-optimized shopping carts, simplified mobile pages, and easier mobile buying experiences into your brand offering, whether you choose to partner with PayPal, Google, or others—or develop your own solutions.

Mobile Advertising

In 2011, Gartner predicted that mobile ad revenue would end the year at US$3.3 billion, skyrocketing to $20.6 billion in 2015, more than doubling each year and continuing to grow thereafter. A Boston Retail Partners survey indicates that about 33% of retailers operate a mobile channel as of early 2012, up from 12% the prior year. Tablets especially offer interesting potential for brand owners' marketing efforts and many brand owners are deeply engaged in understanding how to best leverage this rapidly growing platform.

Search ads and location ads (paid-for positioning on maps and augmented reality[31] apps) are expected to deliver the highest revenue, while video/audio ads are expected to see the fastest growth through 2015. Gartner predicts that brand spending on mobile advertising will grow from 0.5 percent of the total advertising budget in 2010 to over 4 percent in 2015. While still a small chunk of the marketing mix, this reflects a stunning growth rate that is only likely to increase.

Mobile marketing can come in many forms. It can be in the form of coupons or other graphics sent to the mobile phone. It could be advertising that runs along the bottom of mobile sites. It could be triggered coupons or discounts sent based on time or location using rich media, including video. It can also be implemented using pay-per-click (PPC) ads from companies like Google.

If you're doing any kind of advertising, you need to seriously think about adding mobile to the mix.

Mobile Phones and 2D Bar Codes

No discussion about mobile marketing is complete without mentioning 2D barcodes. One of the most popular of these is QR codes, square two-dimensional barcodes that when decoded by the phone, direct its browser to a website or send the phone a text or image message (such as a discount code).

QR codes are showing up on everything from billboards to magazine advertisements and direct mail, email and even vehicles. For example, in New York City, garbage trucks carry a QR Code that leads citizens to information about how to recycle properly. Some of the political campaign buses in the 2012 Presidential campaign featured QR codes on the exterior that led to more information about the candidate and offered an opportunity to contribute to the campaign.

[31]More about augmented reality later!

Philadelphia commuters can do their grocery shopping at a virtual store compliments of Internet grocer Peapod, Coca-Cola and Procter & Gamble's Charmin. Posters at Philadelphia's transit stations feature a variety of commonly purchased grocery items along with QR codes that commuters can scan with a Peapod mobile app for ordering and delivery by Peapod.

QR codes are increasingly found on product labels to provide up-to-the-minute product information, including details about ingredients, product comparisons, coupon offers, recipes and other marketing and informational tactics. With all the contamination scares over produce, consumers want to know the source of the food that they are buying, and QR codes provide any easy way to deliver against this demand.

In its *25 Trendsetters to Watch* issue (January 1, 2012), Chief Marketer commented, "By the numbers, 2011 has probably been the year of the QR Code." In January of 2012, a Consumer Pulse study reported that one in five scanned QR codes initiate a purchase. Researcher Jeff McKennia, senior consultant at Chadwick Martin Bailey, who conducted the study, commented, "Companies need to understand what consumers expect from a scan whether it's more information, a coupon or exclusive offer. Companies who use QR codes successfully to drive engagement or sales will be those who meet customer expectations and offer compelling reasons to scan."

Of course I have some examples for you:

QR codes are being used to solve a "fishy" problem in Boston. According to an October 2011 Boston Globe series of investigative articles on the fish business, DNA testing organized by the Globe revealed nearly half of 183 fish samples collected at restaurants and supermarkets in the Boston area were not the species ordered. To counteract bad publicity and to assure consumers they are actually receiving the species of fish ordered, a company called Trace and Trust, a network of fishermen, distributors, processors and restaurants, organized a system that uses QR codes to track individual fish from the ocean to your plate. Trace and Trust tells customers exactly who caught their seafood, as well as when, where, and how it got caught. The community believes this level of transparency results in the highest quality and freshest possible seafood you have ever seen. Now there's a use for QR codes I bet you never predicted!

One of the biggest users of QR codes is Best Buy. Just walk in the door and QR codes are all around you. Best Buy uses them on all of its major products on display. Scan the code on the product ID card and you'll be taken to a mobile website with access to specs, customer reviews, and more. All of the mobile sites have the same format, creating a brand buying experience that is predictable and highly useful to the shopper. For Best Buy, in many cases, this has replaced generic product barcodes which make it too easy for shoppers to compare Best Buy prices with those of other online and offline vendors as well as to seek alternative and similar products. As mentioned earlier, Best Buy also has a price-matching offer in place to fight against customer defection at point of purchase.

Sears has jumped on the QR code bandwagon, using the codes on out-of-home advertising to enable holiday shoppers to purchase toys directly from their smartphones. Sears calls these ads "mobile shopping walls," and is placing them in high-traffic areas such as airports. The ads showcase the most popular toys, and enable shoppers to purchase while waiting around in airports, malls, movie theaters or bus shelters. This is one way the company is delivering an integrated shopping experience to customers.

GLAMOUR MAGAZINE's September 2011 issue deployed QR codes from provider SpyderLynk that took users to video content, contests and giveaways or to advertisers who were running their own contests. The issue reportedly saw more than a half million reader engagements with the codes, and unique users roughly equating to 4% of *Glamour's* circulation.

In another media mix twist, HSN used QR codes to bridge the gap between broadcast and online, building QR codes into the onscreen product displays so users could scan them for more detailed information. In this case, it was easy for the announcer to explain (probably over and over again!) how to use the QR codes. Full results hadn't been reported at the time of this writing, but we understand that HSN is looking into ways to have code scans load items directly into the user's shopping cart.

Sales pitch alert: For more information on how to generate QR Codes and the best methods for using them, check out QreateAndTrack.com, *QR codes are free to add to your promotional materials, and when used right, offer significant value. They offer another opportunity to reach the mobile audience!*

If you're not actively incorporating QR codes into your marketing programs, you are missing a huge opportunity. Just ask Chili's, whose recent fundraising campaign for childhood cancer resulted in 291,000 scans of QR codes that appeared on coloring sheets and table tents created especially for the effort and raised more than $5 million for the cause. Digital promotions do come with some downsides: You must make sure your staff is aware of what is being offered. A couple years ago, I checked in at Chili's using foursquare and there was a promotion in place that qualified me for a free basket of chips and salsa that I found out about through social media. However, the waiter was completely unaware of the promotion. So whether you are using foursquare, QR Codes, Groupon or any other mobile or social media promotional means, and regardless of the size of your business, make sure your staff is fully up to speed on the latest offers and activities!

In a related sales/marketing application, retailer Old Navy has launched its SnapAppy app that loyal customers can use in a number of ways. It doesn't use QR codes. Rather, it is a specialized application that recognizes the Old Navy's logo and allows consumers who "snap" that logo via the app to unlock deals, games and fashion tips. Shoppers can also purchase items directly from Old Navy's mobile-optimized web site inside the app. While this requires the use of a specialized app—as opposed to a generic QR code reader—it may foreshadow efforts by other retailers to lock in loyal customers who, in exchange for a bit of fun and excitement, are willing to use their branded app to enhance their shopping experience. SnapAppy even includes a click-to-call experience as well as alerts. Although the retailer is making a bigger deal about the value to the customer than it is about the value to Old Navy, it is likely that these transactions are adding significant intelligence to Old Navy's databases as well.

Research by iModerate Research Technologies in October of 2011[32] revealed that half of smartphone owners had scanned a QR Code and nearly 20% of those made a purchase as a result. The biggest driver to actually get the consumer to scan the code, according to the research, was the ability to gain access to discounts, coupons and free items.

While we are on the subject of codes, it bears mentioning that there are other types of barcodes that are useful with mobile devices.

Standard UPC codes can also be read with a barcode scanner. With the right app, such as Google Shopper or Amazon's Price Check, these codes can be read to instantly compare prices. For example, with Amazon Price Check, a shopper could be looking at an item in a retail store, wondering whether he or she was getting the best price. In the past, that might have required poring through a number of catalogs or web sites, or visiting several stores. By scanning the product code, the shopper can get an instant check as to what that item might cost if purchased from Amazon or one of its merchants.

Google Shopper allows you to not only get detailed product information by scanning the product code, but also find prices, reviews and other locations where the product is sold.

During the 2011 holiday season, Amazon offered a $5 credit for shoppers who scanned a code in a retail store and then ultimately purchased the item through Amazon. How many shoppers took advantage of this offer as they stood in frustratingly long lines, or just wanted a better price? It's hard to say, since Amazon is reluctant

[32] *9Things to Know about Consumer Behavior and QR Codes*,iModerate Research Technologies, October 2011.

to release too many specifics about its business. With the release of 2012's numbers, the pundits will certainly be making educated guesses as to how apps like Amazon Price Check or Google Shopper affected overall sales in brick-and-mortar retail stores.

There are other types of 2D barcodes in use, although QR Codes seem to be dominating at the time of this writing. One that should not be dismissed out of hand is Microsoft Tag. Microsoft calls this a High Capacity Color Barcode (HCCB), and it uses clusters of colored (or black & white) triangles instead of the square pixels usually associated with 2D barcodes. They work basically the same as QR codes, although they do require a proprietary reader (which can also read QR Codes). Tag can also integrate Near Field Communications (NFC—more on this later). Like QR Codes, you can access performance and ROI metrics for Tag. Digital watermarks are another new technology. Digimarc is the leader in this arena. Digital watermarks are, "imperceptible to human senses" and "allows users to embed digital information into audio, images, video and printed materials in a way that is persistent, imperceptible and easily detected by computers and digital devices."

This technology is very new and still requires a great deal of education. Digital watermarks, according to Digimarc, "will deliver a wide range of new, rich media experiences to readers and consumers of your printed content." This new technology will be able to monitor broadcasts and internet distribution, manage digital rights and deter counterfeiting and piracy.

Another technology just entering the market as of this writing is Touchcodes from Print Technologics, a German firm. Touchcodes (www.touchcode.de) are a type of electronic barcode that can be read by a touchscreen, such as a smartphone or iPad. It is an invisible electronic code printed on paper, cardboard, film or labels using the offset or flexographic printing process. It is not designed as a variable data element (such as a QR or Tag code can be) and it cannot be produced using inkjet or toner-based printers. The Touchcode is read by simply placing it on the display of an established multi-touch hardware, such as smartphones and tablet computers.

During the usual printing process, conductive material is printed with a clear electronic code between the layers of the media material. Reading devices - such as smartphones, tablets or touchscreens - recognize the code when it is placed on them; the Touchcode software decodes the data and starts the application on the display immediately.

By their very nature, Touchcodes require a special manufacturing process (print) and cannot be copied or duplicated in the same way a QR code can be copied or duplicated, which can be an added security feature.

Some examples include:

- Product tags and labels that contain a Touchcode can be scanned to verify authenticity, cutting down on counterfeiting.
- Similarly, high value items such as tickets to concerts, sporting events, or other activities can have an embedded Touchcode that can be scanned by a smartphone or other touchscreen device at the gate to ensure tickets are valid.
- A Touchcode embedded in a product installation guide could activate a how-to video that will help users better understand the installation process.
- Touchcodes in magazines or other printed publications can be used to link rich media to a story. Perhaps you are perusing an in-flight magazine that is reviewing a travel destination. Simply read the code with your phone or tablet to access a video showing more detail.

Scan to receive the
"Catching up & Getting Mobile" infographic

Augmented Reality

We have referenced augmented reality, so now let's dive into what is.

According to Wikipedia,[33] "**Augmented reality** (AR) is a live, direct or indirect, view of a physical, real-world environment whose elements are augmented by computer-generated sensory input such as sound, video, graphics or GPS data … As a result, the technology functions by enhancing one's current perception of reality."

Augmented reality blurs the line between what is real and what is computer generated by enhancing what we see, hear, and even feel and smell.

While in the larger scheme of things, augmented reality may require special equipment, including small projectors and/or wearable devices that allow you to see augmented content superimposed on the real world, the technology is already being used with mobile devices, albeit to a limited extent as we enter 2013. According to howstuffworks.com, "In the Netherlands, cell phone owners can download an application called Layar that uses the phone's camera and GPS capabilities to gather information about the surrounding area. Layar then shows information about restaurants or other sites in the area, overlaying this information on the phone's screen. You can even point the phone at a building, and Layar will tell you if any companies in that building are hiring, or it might be able to find photos of the building on Flickr or to locate its history on Wikipedia."

Domino's Pizza uses the Blippar app to create an augmented reality experience for consumers in the UK. Domino's uses a six-sheet poster style to grab consumers' attention as they are on the go, reminding them of the tasty hot pizza they can get from Domino's. The posters allow consumers to download deals for their nearest Domino's store

---

[33] December 20,2011

and/or the Domino's mobile ordering app (which is available for the iPhone, iPad and Android). When the posters are viewed through the Blippar app, the features of the six-sheet posters literally jump off the page. The user loads the app and holds the phone up to the poster. Domino's in the UK is heavily using Facebook and Twitter to attract consumers' attention and to educate them about the campaign and also about augmented reality and the Blippar app. If the consumer does not have the Blippar app or chooses not to use it, no worries. The posters show the current "555" deal which consumers can take advantage of.

Augmented reality is probably not something you need to worry about anytime soon in terms of implementation, but it is certainly a trend you should keep an eye on. Or, if you want to be a really leading edge marketer and have investment resources available, dive in today and perhaps benefit from a first-mover advantage. You can find lots more information on augmented reality by Googling the term or visitinghttp://ilink.me/AugReal. You can also get information about the top augmented reality apps for the iPhone by visitinghttp://ilink.me/iApps, or for Android at http://ilink.me/droidApps

Location-Based Services

Location-based services (LBS) are becoming more popular with the availability of on-board GPS systems in mobile devices. It allows applications on those devices to make use of geographic location. Whether you are looking for the nearest Starbucks, you want updated weather information, or you need to find an ATM, LBS allows you to quickly access that data based on your current location. It can also include coupons or other offers that are directed to mobile users based on their proximity to a certain location.

Initially, there was a lot of hype around location-based services such as foursquare that allowed users to "check in" to a location, and by having the most check-ins, to become mayor of that location. However, the Pew Internet & American Life Project found in May of 2011 that while 58% of smartphone users had used some kind of location-based service on their phone, just 12% had checked in somewhere. This has prompted marketers to focus more on checking out than checking in—that is, using location-based services to influence transactions, whether or not it actually gets customers in the physical door.[34]

Deployment of location-based services must be carefully thought out, however. You don't want your customers to feel like you are stalking them. In 2011, a class action suit was filed against a mobile phone manufacturer claiming that the phone was transmitting precise data about the user's location at regular intervals. This was discovered through the use of the AccuWeather mobile app, which, the suit claims, collects location information that is more precise than necessary to provide weather information.

Phone GPS systems can be useful, allowing users to use map and navigation features and find nearby deals and restaurants. But if you are considering an app or marketing campaign that will use GPS data from smartphones, it is wise to ask users' permission to enable tracking before ingesting and acting on any of that data.

Geo-Fencing

Geo-fencing takes LBS to a higher level. A geo-fence is a virtual perimeter for a real-world geographic area. For example, it might be a five-mile radius around a store or restaurant, or a school attendance zone. It can be both a security feature and a marketing tool.

When a location-aware device of a location-based service (LBS) user enters or exits a geo-fence, the device receives and/or sends a notification. That notification will vary, depending on the application being used. It can also generate notifications to other devices that will cause certain actions to take place.

As a security feature, geo-fencing, used with child location services enabled on the child's mobile phone, could notify parents when a child

[34] 2012 Trends: Checking In on Checking Out,eMarketer, November 30, 2011.

leaves a designated area. Other applications include sending an alert if a vehicle is stolen, alerting rangers when wildlife strays into farmland, or even immobilization of equipment that leaves a permitted area.[35] This can apply to company-owned vehicle fleets used by delivery drivers, service technicians, or even outside sales representatives, in order to ensure that mobile employees stay within certain boundaries the company has deemed appropriate for whatever reason. Sounds a little Big-Brother-ish doesn't it? That's why it is important to carefully consider implementing any of these programs for marketing purposes. What you hope to achieve should be carefully balanced with the perception of intrusive technology. And as with any digital program, having folks opt-in is always the safest approach.

The 2011 holiday shopping season was heavily influenced by mobile and geo-fencing played a role as well. Retail real estate company DDR Corp., which owns hundreds of U.S. shopping centers, began using a location-based mobile marketing service at its 27 open-air malls across 16 markets to text deals from the retail tenants within those malls. This obviously was designed to help draw more business to the malls, but also was a tremendous benefit to the smaller businesses in those malls that might not have had the resources or know-how to do this themselves.

DDR used Placecast as the foundation of a branded application called ValuText for this initiative. Placecast was founded in 2005 on the belief that both place and time are the universal keys to relevance in the mobile experience. The Placecast platform is built with location and time at the core in order to resolve the complex data, relevancy, and scaling issues of running location-based programs for large audiences across any connected device. Placecast ShopAlerts is an opt-in service that more than a million consumers have opted into.

ShopAlerts uses geo-fencing to deliver relevant text or rich media messages from retailers or other businesses when a customer is within a determined radius of the business. Placecast reports that in prior

---

[35]Source: Wikipedia, December 17, 2011.

campaigns, 53% of participating shoppers have visited a specific retailer after receiving a location-based alert and 50% who stopped by a store prompted by a text said the visit was unplanned. Unlike deals-based offerings like Groupon, ShopAlert doesn't require the customer to purchase in advance, and it is easy for businesses to frequently update offers for products and services. With a solution like Groupon, a small business could be so inundated with customers (the flash-mob effect) that they are unable to handle the volume and end up disappointing many would-be customers—not a good thing, since bad news travels fast. With a solution like Placecast ShopAlert, there is more control over how many customers the offer is extended to, the timing and more.

Near Field Communication (NFC)

Another important mobile trend is near field communications. Adoption rate has been slower in the U.S. than in other parts of the world, but it is definitely something to keep your eye on.

Pick up your own copy of the **Ultimate Guide to NFC** at http://ilink.me/Ultimate.

According to Wikipedia,[36] near field communication (NFC) is a set of standards for smartphones and similar devices to establish radio communication with each other by touching them together or bringing them into close proximity, usually no more than a few centimeters. It builds on RFID systems by allowing two-way communication, where early systems, such as smart cards, were one-way only. Present and anticipated applications include contactless transactions, data exchange, and simplified setup of more complex communications such as Wi-Fi. Communication is also possible between an NFC device and an unpowered NFC chip, called a "tag." It even has applications in healthcare delivery. Personal health monitors recording vital data can be read by an NFC reader/writer, such as the person's mobile phone, by simply touching the reader to the health device. Because of the proximity required, healthcare professionals can be assured they have a good understanding of which data is being read at which time, greatly improving patient safety and reducing the chance of human error, mitigating what can be a huge problem in healthcare delivery.

NFC devices can be used in contactless payment systems, similar to those currently used in credit cards and electronic ticket smartcards, and allow mobile payment to replace or supplement these systems. For example, Google Wallet allows consumers to store credit card information in a virtual wallet and then use an NFC-enabled device at terminals that accept MasterCard PayPass transactions. It can also be used in social networking situations for such things as sharing contacts, photos or files, or participating in multiplayer mobile games.

According to a May 2011 article on Wired.com, published just prior to the announcement of Google Wallet, Sarah Clark, editor of *Near Field Communications World*, stated, "NFC could become the industry standard for mobile payments within the next year." Is this another case of an overly optimistic trade publication hyping new technology, or is it real? Good question. One of the biggest challenges will be unseating established payment systems like Visa and MasterCard to bring down transaction costs. Another barrier, at least in the U.S.,

---

[36]December 17, 2011

is the number of smartphones that don't support NFC payments. That is quickly changing, however. As of this writing, Clark's list of phones available today, phones coming soon, and phones rumored includes more than 50 models. Many are not available in the U.S., but some are: the Samsung Galaxy Nexus, the Google Nexus S, and several Blackberry models, to name a few. Rumors persist that future Apple iPhones will feature NFC, but there have been no formal announcements or confirmations from the company. Microsoft has confirmed that the Windows Phone operating system will offer NFC in 2012, as well as support for NFC in Windows 8.[37]

Estimates show between 35 million to 45 million NFC-enabled mobile phones were shipped worldwide in 2011—a small percentage of overall shipments, but still significant. This includes phones from Nokia, Samsung and RIM—but not Apple. Because penetration is still so small, it will take time to grow to critical mass. Not only do buyers need to be convinced to purchase phones with NFC capability, but they also have to change behaviors at point of payment. Perhaps the larger issue is the investments that retailers need to make in point-of-sale readers—especially with an economy that is not growing robustly, retailers are likely to put off these investments for the near term. So it becomes somewhat of a chicken-and-egg scenario. In the end, we believe NFC will become a standard payment technology, and it is important for marketers and others to stay current with developments.

From the consumer perspective, this transformation will be driven not so much by payment convenience, according to many experts, but by value wrapped around the experience, such as enabling consumers to discover offerings via contextualized coupons and to explore new product and service information. This approach also enables companies to engage with customers by providing loyalty points and rewards subsequent to a product purchase.[38]

---

[37]See www.NFCworld.com/nfc-phones-list/#available for updated information on NFC-enabled phones

[38]*Product Strategists Should See NFC As Much More Than Contactless Payments,* by Thomas Husson, Forrester, Paid Content, December 19, 2011.

To stay current with NFC developments, we recommend monitoring the NFC Forum (www.nfc-forum.org), formed to advance the use of NFC technology by developing specifications, ensuring interoperability among devices and services, and educating the market about NFC technology.

Mobile Operating Systems

Before we talk about tablets, another significant development in the world of untethered communications, it makes sense to spend some time talking about mobile operating systems—not in exacting detail, but in enough depth that you understand the basics.

As mentioned earlier, there are two leading operating systems in the worlds of smartphones and tablets: Apple's iOS and Google's Android. RIM's Blackberry and Windows Mobile are smaller players that won't be addressed in detail here. (Who would have thought one would say Microsoft is a smaller player?) But in this case, they were late to the game. The game is not yet over, though, so if you happen to be a Microsoft fan, there is hope. At the end of 2011, Microsoft announced that it had reached 50,000 apps in its Windows 7 Phone Marketplace.

There is so much hoopla over Apple's entry to these markets, that one would think iOS is the dominating operating system, but one would be wrong.

According to comScore, one in ten mobile subscribers owned an iPhone in September of 2011,just before the iPhone 4S was released. The top smartphone manufacturers, Samsung, LG and Motorola (being acquired by Google as this is being written), have 25.3%, 20.6% and 13.8% market share respectively. These phones, however, all use Google's Android operating system, and that platform has nearly a 50% market share.

One month later, Millennial reported Android's lead as the most popular platform on its mobile advertising network, as indicated in the chart below. This is further encouragement for developers to focus their efforts on both the Android and Apple platforms.

Figure 3. Connected Device and Smartphone OS Mix

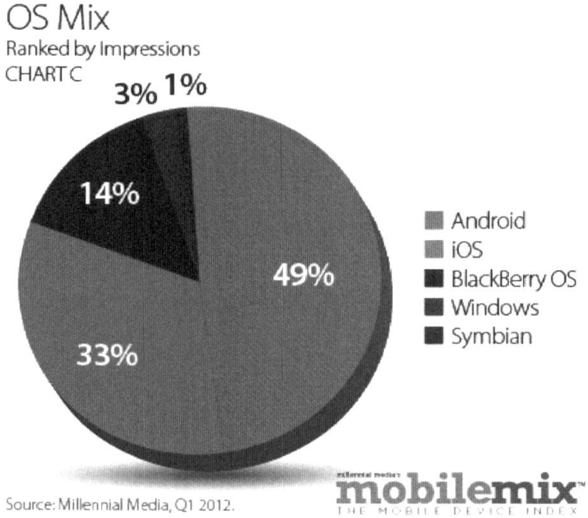

These numbers continue to shift, of course. On Christmas Day, 2011, Flurry Analytics found that 6.8 million Android and iOS devices (smart phones and tablets) were activated, with Google reporting that 3.7 million of those were Android devices. Check our resource page untetheredmarketing.com for updated statistics as they become available.

Do you remember life before your smartphone? Odds are, you owned something known as a feature phone. A feature phone, as defined by Wikipedia as a, "low-end mobile phone that has less computing ability than a smartphone."

According to comScore, more than 110 million people in the United States owned a smartphone in June of 2012. Nielsen reported that just about half of all US mobile phone subscribers in February 2012 owned smartphones. It is projected that by the end of 2014, a feature phone will be very hard to find, as smartphones will have a very firm grasp of the market.

Not convinced that smartphones are the wave of the future? Sony Ericsson already has plans to axe their feature phone line and concentrate on making smartphones only. Who will be next and do the same?

Apple's iOS is a tightly controlled, closed operating system - long an Apple heritage. The Android operating system is made available to developers at no charge and with few implementation restrictions. Thus, while Android has the largest market share, it is also fragmented in terms of release levels, and features and functions the various smartphone and tablet manufacturers choose to support and implement. Google does appear to be making some moves to gain greater control over this situation.

The market share battle is certainly not over, and the scales are likely to continue to tip one way or another. In the third quarter of 2011, according to Gartner, Android represented 53% of smartphone shipments—some 60 million devices worldwide, increasing by a factor of three from the year before and twice as much market share. Meanwhile, Apple's share dropped—shipments grew overall, but not enough to offset Android's market share grab. Part of this can be attributed to the fact that the release in the fourth quarter of the iPhone 4S was widely anticipated, and Apple aficionados likely postponed purchases. Even with significant iPhone 4S purchases over the holidays, Apple is still not likely to come close to Android's market share.

Apple reported sales of more than four million iPhone 4S units in its first weekend, an Apple record and likely a mobile phone record. But that level of sales may not be sustainable and is a spike that can be attributed to pent-up demand.

Consider the story of my sons and their smartphone usage. Once upon a time, they thought they wouldn't want an iPhone. Now, I don't find myself reminding them about their hockey games anymore, they have a phone that can do that for them.

When they decided to enter the iPhone fray, I told them they could get the iPhone 3. I could buy that phone for $50 and put them on my data plan at a discount. When a new version of the iPhone comes out, the older models decrease in price dramatically. If you are considering getting them a smartphone, get it cheap. It's not the phone they are selling you, it is the subscription and the recurring revenues that rack up the bill.

Check out the next section on Tablets for more details about operating system market share in that segment.

Why is all of this important? It really is not about selling a phone or tablet for a few hundred bucks. It is more about establishing the dominant mobile communications and computing platform for the future, and Google seems to be winning that war handily. Marketshare is critical not only for the revenue it brings to suppliers, but also because these devices rely to a greater or lesser degree, depending on which device you are talking about, on third-party app developers. Those developers are not going to invest valuable resources in developing for a lagging platform. For example, as RIM's place in the market continues to slide, fewer developers are investing in that platform.

It's a slightly different story for the Windows operating system, both for phones and tablets. Microsoft has taken a hard stance on the patent infringement front, forcing some manufacturers who have adopted the Android platform, including HTC and Samsung, to sign cross-licensing agreements in which Microsoft receives a royalty from the sale of their Android devices. Speculation is that one of the key drivers for Google's acquisition of Motorola Mobility is to gain access to its 17,000 patents, which could stand to strengthen its position in the patent wars. It is being attacked not only by Microsoft, but also by Apple, BT, Oracle and a number of patent trolls across a variety of fronts. Estimates are that nearly 100 mobile-related patent cases are in process worldwide at the time of this writing. Time will tell how the patent trolls[39] fare over the long term with respect to mobile devices.

[39]Patent troll: A company or person who buys and enforces patents against one or more alleged infringers in a manner considered by the target or observers as unduly aggressive or opportunistic, often with no intention to further develop, manufacture or market the patented invention. While Microsoft and Apple are not patent trolls in the sense of buying patents for this purpose (it has plenty of its own), they have certainly been aggressive.

Tablets, Tablets Everywhere, Even in the Air

So far, we have been focusing on smartphones as a key enabler of untethered operations, but tablets also play a significant role. As with smartphones, the tablet market is on fire—and this is not a pitch for the Kindle Fire, just a statement of fact.

On the tablet side, the launch of the Apple iPad on January 27, 2010, rocked the geek (and general consumer) world. Using the same operating system as the iPhone, this tablet computer, in a 10-inch form factor, will only run programs approved by Apple and distributed via the Apple App Store (with the exception of programs that run within the browser)—in short, a closed system. The company sold three million iPads in its first 80 days and 14.8 million during 2010, representing 75% of tablet sales that year. As of September 2011, some 40 million iPads had been sold, with an expectation that the company would sell 13.5 million more units in the fourth quarter of 2011. On Black Friday 2011, Apple was reportedly selling some 14.8 iPads per hour at its retail stores, up from 8.8 iPads per hour the year before![40]

RIM's Blackberry Playbook, a 7-inch form factor tablet using the RIM operating system, has not done well. According to an IDC survey of 2,000 developers worldwide,[41] RIM ends the year with less than 1% of the global tablet market share.

Other tablet entries include:

- Samsung Galaxy Tab (7-inch and 10-inch form factors),
- Motorola Xoom (10"),
- Acer Iconia (10"),
- Asus Slider and Transformer (10"),
- Asus MeMo (7"),

[40]Source: *Relax—iPad sales are doing just fine*, by Larry Dignan, CNET News, November 28, 2011

[41]*Appcelerator/IDC Mobile Developer Report, November 2011*

• LG G-Slate (9"),

• Kindle Fire (7"),

• HTC (Flyer (7"),

• Jetstream (10")

• EVO View 4G (7")

All of these are Android based.

The Google Nexus also debuted in 2012, a tablet that is a complete Google product. It incorporates Google Play, Gmail, Chrome, Google+ and YouTube.

Dell is one company that hasn't done that well in tablet world. The Dell Streak 7" tablet came to market early with good reviews, but Dell's site states it is no longer available online. Dell also came to market with the Streak 5, a 5" tablet/smartphone combo, which it has also pulled from the market. Its Inspiron duo, billed as "the new convertible," had a flip hinge that allowed users to seamlessly switch from touch to type. That one is gone, too, replaced by laptops. The company now seems to be focusing its efforts on laptops, desktops, servers and phones.

New to the market in November of 2011 was the Kindle Fire, also Android based. It was a game-changer, the first tablet to offer a true challenge to the iPad. Although Amazon does not release specific unit numbers, estimates were it would sell 3.9 million Kindle Fires during the 2011 holiday season. And the company did report, in mid-December of 2011, that for the third week in a row, customers were purchasing well over a million Kindle devices per week, with the Kindle Fire remaining the number one bestselling, most gifted and most wished-for product across the millions of items available on Amazon.com since its introduction. Priced at $199 compared to the $500 or so price tag for the iPad and other tablets (depending on model), the Kindle Fire puts tablet computing within easy range for more buyers. It may have less functionality, but for many buyers, this is obviously not that important. More on this later.

ABI Research notes between April and June of 2012, tablet vendors shipped nearly 25 million units and "on track to exceed 100 million units" before 2012 is said and done.[42]

Tablets: Not a New Concept

The concept of tablet computing has been around for decades. Just watch this 1994 video produced by newspaper publisher Knight Ridder at http://ilink.me/Tablet94. Called The Tablet Newspaper: A Vision of the Future, it predicted a world in which "people carry around portable computing devices that will 'weigh under two pounds,' have a display 'comparable to ink on paper,' and will be able to 'blend text, video, audio and graphics.'" Timing was off by almost a decade, though. The Boulder, Colorado, think tank that dreamed this up predicted it would happen by the turn of the century. Too bad newspapers didn't sit up and take notice in 1994 … they could have saved themselves a lot of grief by starting a little earlier with the digital thing. The concept was that people would use computers to create information, but use the tablet to interact with information: reading, watching, listening. It turns out that tablets do a whole lot more than envisioned back then, of course, and are used to create content. In fact, Morgan Stanley reports that 20% of tablet owners use the device to edit or create files regularly. I certainly do.

Personally, I use the iPad as an optional device. I don't rely on it as much as my iPhone, but it offers a larger display to get work done and run applications. Some of those apps are ones that generally don't exist for laptop use, e.g., tools like the Around Me application that I wouldn't have access to on a tethered computer. The iPad is also great for business convenience, allowing me to access information that makes my travel experience much easier.

---

[42]http://news.yahoo.com/ipad-demand-push-tablet-shipments-past-100-million-014516477.html

Even if I just want to play solitaire or blackjack or read a book, those are made much easier on a tablet. Having an iPhone and iPad also allows me to move back and forth between devices while seeing the same content.

The iPad is great for presenting as well. It shows I have adapted to new technology and can offer an impressive and effective presentation. One downside, at least for me, is that I am more comfortable with an actual keyboard than the virtual keyboard on a tablet or smartphone. When it comes to manipulating apps and heavy content presenting, it becomes more cumbersome.

I don't type all of my emails on my smartphone, but the tablet, when equipped with an external keyboard, becomes a more feasible option. The iPad can even function as a television. Buy a little tool called a Slingbox and place it on top of your cable box at home. Connect it to your TV and high speed internet. Get the corresponding app on your phone or iPad and that's all it takes. You can watch your favorite TV shows on the go, anywhere, anytime.

The idea goes back even farther: Remember the Apple Newton? In fact, as rumors of an Apple tablet began to emerge before the iPad came out, it was reported that Apple had hired back a Newton PDA developer. In the late 1980's, John Sculley was running Apple. During his tenure, Sculley envisioned a tablet the size of an opened magazine and did some video mockups of a product he called Knowledge Navigator.[43] That evolved into a project called Newton, named because Apple's original logo had a rendering of Isaac Newton sitting beneath an apple tree. Both the Newton and the Knight Ridder prototype used a stylus instead of fingers on a touch screen. The Newton was supposed to have a ship date of April 2, 1992, and cost less than $1,500. It was a long and rocky road to the Newton's ultimate launch at Macworld Boston in August of 1993 as the MessagePad, but the first 5,000 units sold out (at $800 each) within hours. By that time, other companies, including a British company, Armstrad, were also developing and marketing similar products. Palm came to market with a smaller

---

[43] *The Story Behind Apple's Newton*, by Tom Hormby, Gizmodo, January 19, 2010

shirt pocket size PalmPilot that sold for under $400. Although Apple supposedly had a similar pocket-sized device in its plan, it was never brought to market. Apple, now back under Steve Jobs, officially killed the product in February of 1998. You can read an interesting obituary, full of rumor and speculation, published in Pen Computing Magazine in June of 1998.[44]

Tablets in the Air

Any frequent traveler expects (and most of us dread) the instruction to turn off and stow all electronic devices. We wonder if they truly have any negative impact on navigation. Or maybe airlines and the FAA are more worried about these devices flying around the cabin in case of an accident during take-off or landing. Or maybe it is just a giant conspiracy to keep unruly travelers under their respective thumbs. Who knows? Once in the air, you need to keep the wireless features turned off … unless, of course, you are in a WiFi-equipped plane, of which there are an increasing number, and you cough up the $9.99 fee for the pleasure of staying in touch. For me, it's worth every penny.

But all of this could be changing soon. In December 2011, American Airlines notified customers that certain transcontinental and international flights would be featuring 10" Samsung Galaxy Tab for personal entertainment in first/business class. That announcement was followed closely by the revelation that American Airlines pilots could carry and use iPads in the cockpit—up to two, to eliminate unwieldy paper documentation which they were still using. That generated a great deal of talk. Here you have tablet computers operating at will within inches of supposedly sensitive electronic equipment and yet us folks in the back of the plane have to turn ours off? Go figure.

Time will tell how all of this pans out. We will be patient, because after all, we don't want to be the ones whose heavy wireless activity brings a plane down. Heaven forbid.

---

[44] *Why Did Apple Kill the Newton?*, Pen Computing Magazine, June 1998 (pencomputing.com/frames/newton_obituary.html)

Kindle Fire: A Game-Changer?

The much-awaited Kindle Fire finally began shipping in November of 2011 to mixed reviews from the tech community. Steve Wildstrom of Techpinions.com called it "the most divisive product of 2011." It's not perfect in its first iteration—few products are.

The bottom line with the Kindle Fire is its $199 price tag. This brings it into a range that the average consumer will spring for—and they are, in record numbers. Although Amazon doesn't release specific sales numbers, the company did report, as mentioned earlier, that it was selling more than a million Kindles per week, and the intimation was that most of those were Kindle Fires. Amazon may be losing money on the devices—some experts estimate a $10 loss per unit—but obviously plans to make it up with other revenue based on its huge content library and even larger online shopping mall. There are also significant incentives for Kindle Fire owners to pony up $79 per year to become Amazon Prime members, not only getting free shipping on many things Amazon, but also qualifying for free streaming of thousands of videos—movies, TV shows and more. None of this is hampered by the device's 7-inch form factor.

The other consideration here is that Amazon has proven it is prepared to disrupt its own cash cows. That's what the original Kindle did for printed books. But in exchange, it has what may be the first true media tablet, focused on the future of all media: TV, movies, books, music, magazines, even newspapers.[45] Will the Kindle Fire become the dominant media reader and Amazon the dominant digital media retailer? Time will tell. It certainly seems to be heading that way. And if anyone can pull this off, it is Amazon. The company is smart to take a different path and not try to be an iPad me-too, as other tablet manufacturers seem to be doing.

The Kindle Fire will be a success as long as people understand it is not an iPad, but a media reader with cool apps and a bunch of other

---

[45] *Amazon's Kindle Tablet Will Be The First True Media Tablet*, by Ian Fogg, Paid Content, September 27, 2011.

functionality that could not easily be deployed on its black & white Kindle predecessors. Video quality is great, and surfing the web is fast. You can send email, watch movies or listen to music. It has neither a camera nor geolocation software, another diversion from the strategy of Apple and other tablet makers. And it is wireless only, with no 3G connectivity, at least in its early form. While it may pull some buyers away from an iPad, it is really not an iPad competitor, per se. It is directed at an entirely different audience.

Based on the Android operating system, and using the Amazon-proprietary Silk browser, the device can store up to 8 GB of data. In addition, Amazon gives users 5 GB of cloud storage for free to store videos, music, photos and documents in the Amazon Cloud Drive, with more storage available for a fee. Amazon Silk is powered by the cloud and is sometimes called a "split browser," because some of the activity happens on the device, some in the cloud. This serves two purposes: First, it makes operation faster; and secondly, it keeps the cost of the device lower than if the entire browser software and activity were taking place locally. The potential downside is that all web browsing goes through Amazon before reaching the rest of the Internet, and that might cause some privacy concerns. To address this, Amazon has included a setting that allows disabling of this feature.

Like Apple, Amazon has its private App Store that requires developers to submit apps for approval, a divergent path from the open Android ecosystem where such approvals are not required. Again, Amazon does include an advanced setting that allows acquisition and downloading of non-approved apps, but its use is discouraged, although not prohibited.

That being said, developers are jumping on board at lightning speed. An IDC survey[46] of 2,000 developers worldwide reflected that among the 15 Android tablets on the market at the time, "the low cost, content-rich eReader was second only to the Samsung Galaxy Tab globally in developer interest."

---

[46]*Appcelerator/IDC Mobile Developer Report,* November 2011.

Not Just for Consumers

Tablets are not just toys for consumers. Enterprises are adopting tablets as well, at a much faster rate than expected. Two-thirds of the 50 CIOs that participated in a January 2011 Morgan Stanley survey expected either to purchase tablets for some of their employees or allow employee-owned tablets onto their networks within one year, up from 29% who currently were doing so at the time of the survey.

We'll talk about some of the more popular business (and consumer) tablet (and smartphone) apps in Chapter Four.

Mobile Best Practices

There are many different types of mobile marketing out there today. SMS, apps, mobile websites, location-based marketing, near field communication, QR codes, mobile ads and more fill our smartphones on a regular basis.

When you are deciding on your mobile strategy, there are certain practices you should always abide by. First, be concise. No one wants to read the next great American novel on their smartphone when they are just looking for a quick bit of information. In a similar vein, be cognizant that aesthetics take a back seat to functionality on a mobile platform. Your HTML email blasts may look great when opened on a laptop, but they could fall flat on an iPhone.

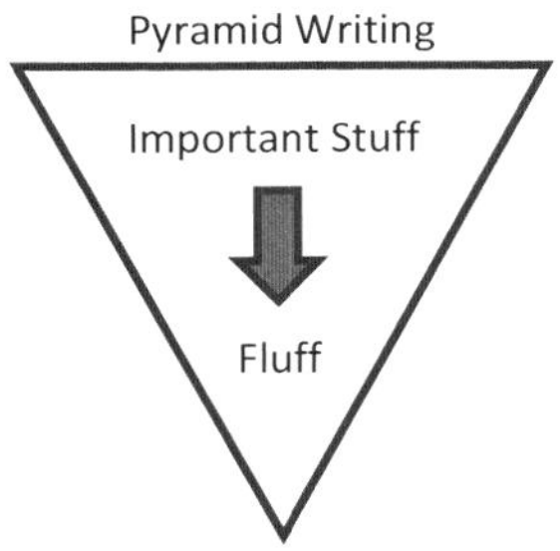

Mobile users are busy and aren't going to wait around for a clunky, slow-loading site. Your mobile site should be optimized to fit to the small screen, quick to load and easy to consume.

Like any other marketing channel, be prepared to capture data from the audience and measure your efforts.

Also keep in mind the inherent link between mobile and social media. The statistics on social media access via smartphones are staggering. 26% of U.S. consumers access social networks on mobile as of August 2012.[47] More time is spent on social networks on mobile devices than computers.[48] A Google study released in early September 2012 noted that 66% of social media access begins on a smartphone.[49]

Long story short, integrate your social media channels into your mobile presence. Your prospects and customers are there – you should be as well.

Get Out and Get Mobile!

Mobile might be a brave new world for many marketers, but it's one worth getting into.

- It's fast.
- It connects you with your customers immediately.
- It's effective.

Cost of entry is low and using solutions like iFlyMobi, and QReate& Track, it's becoming easier all the time.

What are you waiting for? Get out there and get mobile!

In the next chapter, we will delve into the role of apps in mobile marketing for both tablets and phones, exploring how companies are leveraging them to gain brand recognition, educate customers and increase sales. You may be surprised at how easy it is to create your own apps, and we will talk about that, too.

---

[47]http://techcrunch.com/2012/08/08/emarketer-26-of-u-s-consumers-access-social-networks-on-mobile-today-facebook-85-of-that/

[48]http://news.cnet.com/8301-1023_3-57429653-93/smartphones-beat-computers-for-facebookers-time-on-site/

[49]http://www.mobilemarketer.com/cms/news/research/13681.html

Chapter Four: There's an App for That!

This chapter, building on the previous chapters, will get you geared up for mobile, and will also help you understand the synergy between mobile communications/marketing and other media, including web, print and broadcast. So let's talk about apps.

Mobile app is shorthand for mobile application, a term used to describe Internet applications that run on smartphones, tablets and other mobile devices.

Online tech blogger SlashGear reported that Christmas Day 2011 saw the download of 242 million apps; 1.2 billion apps were downloaded in the week between Christmas and New Year's. So whatever they are, apps are a big deal! Let's dig in.

Mobile apps can make it easier for users to utilize the Internet on mobile devices and to perform specific activities. Keep in mind, there is a distinction between web apps that are built for a mobile device and mobile apps that are created for very defined actions. And just to keep you on your toes a bit more, remember that there are crucial differences between the tablet and smartphone deployments.

Let's break it down. Web apps are tools that you access over the internet. As phones evolve, consumers want to access the internet from their mobile phones. The phones need web browsers. But even with a browser, there's a problem. The speed of wireless isn't fast enough to handle the web apps properly. The reality is high speed internet on your desktop or laptop is different than mobile wireless.

We won't get too much in the weeds here, but I know you've heard the terms "3G" and "4G." Is 4G faster than 3G? You bet. But it's not as fast as you think. In fact, it's only about 3-5x faster…not some sort of lightning speed that perhaps the mobile phone companies want you to believe. At least not in terms of web data. In time, as smartphones speed up, you may see web apps gaining some ground. But for now, phones really need mobile apps that are designed to work on phones and provide a very specific experience to the user.

Some mobile apps aren't even that sophisticated, but they serve the designed purpose. For instance, let's say you download a conference app onto your phone so you can experience a conference on the go, rather than being tied to your desktop or laptop computers. Some of that data resides on the phone, sort of like having a client server.

The bottom line is that the experience with a mobile app must be different. Not only is the user dealing with a much smaller screen, but also with a slower data stream. But as technology evolves, who knows how far we may come? Remember back to the days of dial-up? And now, it's all about FIOS or cable in our homes.

The advertising model, as we have come to understand it, is broken. The unwritten agreement between the consumer and the creator of content has been altered. There are people on eBay who run stores but have never sold a product. They are all drop shipped from someone else. Virtual, untethered businesses can operate from anywhere.

We have already discussed some of the apps that have been developed by various retailers, including the Walgreen's/Winn Dixie pharmacy app, Old Navy's SnapAppy, and shopping apps used by Best Buy, Sears, Kohl's and others. Some additional examples of mobile apps for business and personal use include the list below. Some may be useful to your business, while others may give you ideas of apps you could develop that will be useful to your business:

- Square is an app that uses a small magnetic strip reader which plugs into the smartphone audio port and allows swiping of credit cards. Square charges a 2.5% fee for each transaction, with funds transferred directly to the user's specified bank account. With Square, there is no need to establish a merchant account as is the case with most credit card transaction processing systems. Card information can be manually entered as well.

- iTap mobile allows you to securely manage a Windows desktop from your iPhone, iPad or Android device, or a Mac or Linux computer using Remote Desktop Protocol (RDP). See our skydiving story in Chapter Five for one way we have used this helpful app.

- iClickr Power Point Remote (available for iOS, Android and Windows) allows you to use your mobile device to control a PowerPoint presentation being projected from your Mac or Windows PC. You can see either the slide or notes view of the presentation on your handheld device. You can also change slides, change slide presentations, put up a blank screen and more. Why would you ever want to do a PowerPoint presentation any other way?

- Google Shopper is available for both Android and iPhone and contains a wide range of functionality that makes mobile shopping easier, including daily and nearby offers, built-in barcode scanning to find or learn more about almost any product, price comparisons, search by voice, and the ability to share finds with friends.

- American Airlines has an app that lets users verify flight schedules and status, reservations, and for Advantage members, review the status of their account. It also allows flight check-in and displays boarding passes on the phone's screen, eliminating the need for a paper boarding pass. Most airlines offer a similar app.

- Adobe Carousel allows you to access and manipulate your entire photo library from your iPad, iPhone and Mac without syncing. Adobe has a number of other mobile apps in its portfolio as well.

- You can subscribe to various newspapers and magazines via your smartphone and/or tablet. For each publication, you must download and/or purchase an app. For example, if you want to view the Wall Street Journal on a mobile device, you can download a free app that allows you to view the headlines and first sentence or so of each article. Reading the full article requires a paid subscription. This is called the freemium model, which emerged in the mobile app market in 2011. In fact, 65% of Android Marketplace revenue comes from the freemium model.

- Papa John's pizza chain has launched apps for both Android and Apple that allow consumers to browse the entire menu, take advantage of all online coupons and special offers, and of course, actually order their food. The app enables the hungry consumer to pay via cash, credit card, and in some locations, checks. Consumers can also use the app to locate the nearest Papa John's. This type of app is likely to become increasingly common in the restaurant business to make ordering, reservations and other actions more convenient for busy consumers.

- Office supplies retailer Staples is having success with a tablet-optimized app and reports that traffic from tablet devices grew faster than traffic from smartphones. One example of what the app can do is it allows consumers to find printer ink with only three screen touches. How many times have you wandered through an office supply store like a lost puppy, ending up in front of the huge array of printer ink cartridges trying to figure out—or even remember—exactly which one works for your printer?

- All platforms feature tons of game apps—ranging from Temple Run to Angry Birds to Words with Friends—the list goes on and on. Although your company is probably not going to be developing the next hot mobile game, I bring up games because they can be useful as promotional apps. Think creatively about how a simple game app or sweepstakes app might be used to hook people in, educate them about your products or services in a fun and innovative way, and maybe even get them to buy something. And with apps getting easier to develop, this is not as much of a stretch as you might think.

- Sports Tap is another app that is not business related—unless you run a sports team or league. It gives sports fans access to sports scores, stats and more from their mobile device. It can also mean that an employee can get this information—which is important to him—quickly and without too much disruption to the work process. So there is that angle as well.

- SlingPlayer is another cool app. It works with a device (Slingbox) connected to your home television and it allows you to watch your home TV from anywhere. Of course, if someone else is watching that same device in your living room (preferably a family member), you will have to watch what they are watching. But it is a nice way to keep up with the latest news and your favorite soaps (just kidding) from anywhere you are in the world. This can be convenient, especially if you are traveling in a different country where most of the TV is either in the native language, or you can't get the news you need.

- Yelp is a very popular website that provides reviews and recommendations for restaurants, shopping, nightlife, entertainment, services and more. Traveling in a strange town and need to take a client to lunch? Yelp it. Have some sort of equipment failure on the road and need to find the nearest place to get it fixed? Yelp it. You get the idea. Yelp also has a mobile app, as you would expect, so you don't have to boot up that clunky laptop to get the information you need.

- Waze is a free social mobile app that enables drivers to build and use live maps, real-time traffic updates and turn-by-turn navigation for an optimal commute. It makes your phone into a GPS, and it is 100% powered by users. It is constantly updated as users drive around with the app open on their phones. If they are stuck in traffic, that gets noted so you can take an alternative route. Users can also report such things as potholes, construction, map errors, incorrect road signs or other obstacles to a smooth travel experience. (Wisely, typing is disabled while your vehicle is moving.) This is a great tool for anyone who has to either commute or drive to business meetings. It will help make sure you have the best possible chance of being on time, and the least possible chance of wasting time and being unproductive and frustrated.

- Remember the Milk is an online to-do list that is everywhere you are, on your desktop, phone or tablet. No more sticky notes or scribbled lists, and no worries about which device you are actually using at any given time. The basic app is free; an upgrade to Pro is available. You can also sync the app to Outlook, BlackBerry or your Gmail account or Google calendar. (Syncing with Outlook and BlackBerry require an upgrade to Pro).

- Instagram is free a photo sharing app. Simply snap a photo with your phone, choose a filter to transform the look and feel (optional), and send it to Facebook or Flickr.

- Postagram makes it easy to send a printed Instagram photo in the mail. The photo itself is die cut to allow easy removal at the recipient's discretion. What a great way to follow up a sales activity or customer visit! Snap a photo of the customer's building, logo sign, or the customer herself (with permission, of course), and as you are on your way out to your car or before you even leave the parking lot, send a thank-you note that is the ultimate in personal communications. Auto dealers and other purveyors of high-end products can also use this tool. Take that photo of the prospect standing next to the latest Lexus or BMW, and make it into a postcard encouraging them to come back and buy … or if they already bought, remind them to come for recommended service using the optional 140 character message feature. Each Postagram is personalized with the Instagram profile photo of the sender. The uses are endless. You can have fun with it with family and friends, too, of course! Each Postagram is printed and delivered anywhere in the world for 99 cents. What a deal!

- In addition to Remember the Milk, there are a number of productivity apps you can explore, including DocumentsToGo, Dragon Dictation, CardStar (manages digital versions of your plastic loyalty, rewards and club membership cards), and Google Docs.

Consumer products companies are also turning to mobile apps and social media to engage directly with customers. This was difficult before, when they had to rely on mass media, in-store advertising, free-standing inserts and the like.

One company who has been leading this charge is Kraft Foods. In addition to garnering a record-setting number of Facebook likes for its Oreo product (what's not to like about Oreos?), its Kraft Mac and Cheese Twitter campaigns, and its Philly Cream Cheese recipe books, it has also launched a smartphone app, the Kraft iFood Assistant. A paid app at 99 cents, it allows users to access Kraft's in-house recipe content, build shopping lists on the phone (including scanning UPC codes in the family pantry before heading out to the store), share recipes on Facebook and link mobile coupons to their grocery loyalty cards. It is estimated that 60% of those who downloaded the app use it regularly, and it was ranked by Apple as one of the most useful smartphone apps of 2011.

Games are also popular mobile apps, and there are both free and paid varieties. Interestingly, a recent study by Xylogic[50] reveals that iPhone users are more likely to use games while Android users are more likely to use other types of apps.

Figure 4.Top Downloads in December 2012

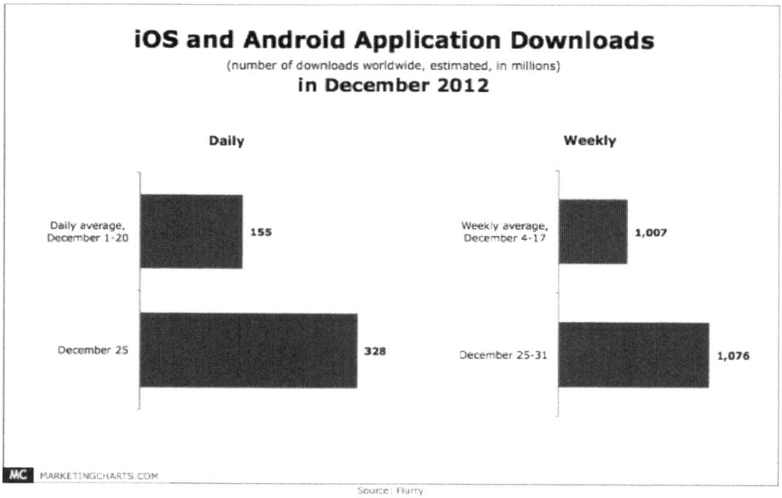

In November of 2011, the top iOS download was Words With Friends Free with more than 3 million downloads (you may remember actor

[50]Source: ReadWrite Mobile. Study: Apps are for Android, Games for the iPhone, by Dan Rowinski, December 22, 2011.

Alec Baldwin being so engrossed in this game as the flight he was on was trying to depart that he refused to turn off his phone and got kicked off the plane). By contrast, there was only one game in the top 10 on Android in the same month, Defender by Droid, with 1.4 million downloads. The top Android download was Facebook for Android, with more than five million downloads.

You might question why you should care about mobile apps if so many people are just using them to play games. This ignores a crucial, unstoppable trend that new technology has caused. The fact of the matter is that apps can and do have significant value and can play an important role in the marketing mix. While game and leisure apps such as Google Maps and email are popular, there are many fabulous business-related apps being developed every day. The only limit to what you can do seems to lie with your imagination. Before you dismiss this option out of hand as too expensive or not worth your while, consider the information presented in this chapter, including examples, stories and tips about how to actually develop these things. The development process is easier than you think. And this increasingly mobile lifestyle is certainly a wave of the future that is already crashing down on us.

As of the end of December 2011, there were one million app titles for mobile devices available in the seven major app stores, according to Distimo, although some of those are the same titles developed for different platforms.

ABI Research predicted that there would be 29 billion apps downloaded in 2011, up from 9 billion in 2010. In the second quarter of 2011, Android overtook Apple in terms of app downloads, with 44% of downloads compared to Apple's 31%, although the Apple App Store generated more revenue than the Android Market.

Download stats can be misleading, however. A January 2010 study by Localytics found that one in four mobile apps, once downloaded, are never used again. Downloads are useful to track, but more important is the tracking of ongoing usage of the app to gauge is usefulness and effectiveness. (And yes, we will discuss tracking towards the end of this chapter).

Canalys predicted in June 2011 that direct revenue from the sale of apps, in-app purchases and subscriptions across smartphones and tablets would be $7.3 billion in 2011, rising to $36.7 billion by 2015.

Interested in more global mobile and app statistics? mobiThinking has a terrific compendium that is kept updated and can be found at http://ilink.me/MobiStats

App Stores

There are seven major app stores where mobile apps can be purchased:

- Amazon Appstore
- Apple App Store for iPad
- Apple App Store for iPhone
- RIM App World
- Google Android Market
- Nokia Ovi Store
- Windows 7 Phone Marketplace

Let's take a closer look at the two largest, Apple and Android.

Apple App Store

In the Apple App Store, for both iPad and iPhone, every product must first be registered with the App Store through iTunes Connect. This means providing a name, description and pricing, as well as other metadata used by the App Store and the application. All Apple App Store products, whether free or paid, must be approved by Apple prior to being available for download. Apple states that the app approval process "is in place to ensure that applications are reliable, perform as expected and are free of explicit and offensive material."[51] Apple provides App Review Guidelines to help developers through this process.

---

[51]https://developer.apple.com/news/

When developing apps, it is important to build time into the launch process for this review to take place. Expedited reviews can be requested, but there are no guarantees that those requests will be honored. Unscientific surveys of app developers indicate an average review time is five days, but in reality it could—and often does—take longer. Developers who choose to create apps for Apple's ecosystem are charged $99 annually for the privilege. Apple does exercise tight control over app approval and approval can be denied for various reasons.

The Apple App Store supports many types of products:[52]

- **Consumable** products must be purchased each time the user needs that item. For example, one-time services are commonly implemented as consumable products.

- **Non-consumable** products are purchased only once by a particular user. Once a non-consumable product is purchased, it is provided to all devices associated with that user's Apple ID. There is built-in support to restore non-consumable products on multiple devices.

- **Auto-Renewable** subscriptions are delivered to all of a user's devices in the same way as non-consumable products. However, auto-renewable subscriptions differ in other ways. When you create an auto-renewable subscription in iTunes Connect, you choose the duration of the subscription. The App Store automatically renews the subscription each time its term expires. If the user chooses to not allow the subscription to be renewed, the user's access to the subscription is revoked after the subscription expires. Your application is responsible for validating whether a subscription is currently active and can also receive an updated receipt for the most recent transaction.

- **Free Subscriptions** are a way for you to put free subscription content in Newsstand. Once a user signs up for a free

[52]Source: Mac OS X Developer Library

subscription, the content is available on all devices associated with the user's Apple ID. Free subscriptions do not expire and can only be offered in Newsstand-enabled apps.

- **Non-Renewing Subscriptions** are an older mechanism for creating products with a limited duration; consider using auto-renewable subscriptions instead. Non-Renewing Subscriptions differ from auto-renewable subscriptions in a few key ways:
  - The term of the subscription is not declared when you create the product in iTunes Connect; your application is responsible for providing this information to the user. In most cases, you would include the term of the subscription in the description of your product.
  - Non-Renewing Subscriptions may be purchased multiple times (like a consumable product) and are not automatically renewed by the App Store. You are responsible for implementing the renewal process inside your application. Specifically, your application must recognize when the subscription has expired and prompt the user to purchase the product again.
  - You are required to deliver non-renewing subscriptions to all devices owned by the user. Non-Renewing Subscriptions are not automatically synchronized to all devices; you must implement this infrastructure yourself. For example, most subscriptions are provided by an external server; your server would need to implement a mechanism to identify users and associate subscription purchases with the user who purchased them.

Thirty percent of revenue from the store goes to Apple; 70% goes to the producer of the app.

In December 2011, Fiksu reported that the Apple App Store served up 5.65 million free app downloads *per day* in November, up from 4.91 million in October. Compared to November of 2010, downloads were up 83%.

Android Marketplace

Android Market is a service that makes it easy for users to find and download Android applications to their Android-powered devices, either from the Android Market application on their device or from the Android Market web site (market.android.com). As of January 2012, the Android Marketplace had more than 100,000 active publishers contributing more than 400,000 active apps. About two-thirds of the apps are free.

A note about free: some free apps are full featured; others have a limited feature set that gets users hooked and positions them to buy the full paid app. Other types of free apps include magazines and newspapers; the app is free, but the user must purchase a subscription to access the content.

As discussed earlier, there is less focus on games in the Android Marketplace than in the Apple ecosystem, although games are definitely available. Android developers are not charged for the privilege of submitting apps to the marketplace. Android.com provides developers with access to the Android SDK and a Developer's Guide. The Dev Guide provides a practical introduction to developing applications for Android and documentation about major platform features. It explores the concepts behind Android, the framework for constructing an application, and the tools for developing, testing, and publishing software for the platform.

To publish an application on Android Market, you first need to register with the service using a Google account and agree to the terms of service (licensing). Once you are registered, you can upload your application to the service whenever you want, update it as many times as you want, and then publish it when you are ready. Once published, users can see your application, download it, and rate it. This less restricted environment is a major difference between Apple and Android app marketplaces. Some reviewers believe this leads to lower quality apps on Android Marketplace than in the Apple App Store. However, others appreciate the more open platform Android offers. The jury is out on which model will win out in the end. Google does, however, have some review processes in place and some apps have been banned from the Market, including tethering apps (for some carriers) that share the Internet connection of an Internet-capable mobile phone with other devices—this is due to the fact that they apparently violated terms of service for certain carriers. Another example of a banned app was SpoofApp, a Caller ID spoofing application typically used for prank calling.

Before installing an application, Android Market displays all required permissions. A game may need to enable vibration, for example, but should not need to read messages or access the phonebook. After reviewing these permissions, the user can decide whether to install the application.

In November of 2011, Google added a music store to the Android Market, placing itself in competition with Apple's iTunes and the Amazon Appstore.

A note about the Kindle Fire: Although it is based on the Android operating system, the Kindle Fire draws its apps from the Amazon Appstore, and Amazon has its own processes and procedures for an app to be posted there. It is possible, although discouraged, to change a setting in the Kindle Fire that would allow "non-approved" apps to be added. Developers are paid either 70% of the sale price or 20% of the developer's list price, whichever is greater. The Amazon Appstore was launched in March of 2011 with 3,800 apps. Speculation is that based on Amazon's size and position in the marketplace, it will quickly become larger than the Android Market, which presents an interesting conundrum for Google in the increasingly fragmented Android space. Amazon is notoriously reluctant to reveal specific stats, such as the number of Kindles sold by model. Stats released in early September of 2012 indicated the Appstore had passes the 50,000 app mark.[53]

Despite its marketplace difficulties, RIM's AppWorld seems to be holding its own. The company announced in February of 2012 that it had surpassed the 60,000 app mark, and claims that it is the most

[53]http://www.theverge.com/2012/9/6/3296612/amazon-appstore-for-android-50000-app-count-september-2012

profitable after the Apple App Store. In AppWorld, purchases are charged directly to the buyer's cell phone bill. RIM claims that 13% of App World publishers have earned $100,000 or more.

In-App Purchases: A New Sales Channel

In-App Purchase allows you to embed a store directly within an application. This store can be used to sell additional content and/or products.

In the case of Apple, developers can use Apple's Store Kit framework, which connects to the App Store on the application's behalf to securely process payments from the user. Developers can use In-App Purchase to implement the following scenarios, according to Apple documentation:

- A basic version of your application with additional premium features
- A book reader application that allows the user to purchase and download new books
- A game that offers new environments (levels) to explore
- An online game that allows the play to purchase virtual property

The same revenue split (70/30) applies to in-app sales as to app sales themselves.

In the Android Marketplace, this is referred to as In-App billing. When you use Android Market's in-app billing service to sell an item, Android Market handles all checkout details so your application never has to directly process any financial transactions. Android Market uses the same checkout service that is used for application purchases, so users experience a consistent and familiar purchase flow. As with Apple, the transaction fee for in-app purchases is the same as the transaction fee for application purchases (30%).

No special account or registration is required other than an Android Market publisher account and a Google Checkout Merchant account. The types of in-app billing that can be integrated are much less specifically defined for the Android Marketplace than they are for the Apple App Store. The developer's guide provides specific technical specifications that must be met.

The Role of iTunes in Apple Apps

Apple iTunes began its life in 2001 as a media player program that allowed users to find, purchase, download and play individual songs and to organize digital music files on desktop computers. It has evolved to allow it to manage content on iPods, iPhones, the iPod Touch and the iPad. iTunes is connected to the iTunes Store. Over time, the iTunes Store has added more functionality and now encompasses TV shows, games, audio books, podcasts, movies and ringtones. It is also used to download apps from the Apple App Store. As I am sure you are aware, iTunes revolutionized the business of buying music and has been perhaps the single greatest change agent pushing a business model overhaul for the music industry.

Building Your Own Apps

Before we get into this, do not even consider building apps in lieu of mobile-optimizing your web site. The latter should take precedence.

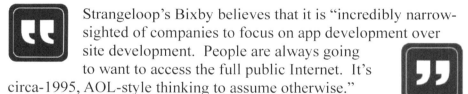

Strangeloop's Bixby believes that it is "incredibly narrow-sighted of companies to focus on app development over site development. People are always going to want to access the full public Internet. It's circa-1995, AOL-style thinking to assume otherwise."

The good news is that you don't have to be a web developer to build your own mobile apps. There are a number of easy-to-use app builders available in the market—and surely more to come—that make your experimentation with mobile app creation affordable. Of course, you must still register with the various App stores to post your content there.

In the early days of mobile apps (what, two or three years ago?), if you wanted to create an app, you had to actually create each different version for each platform. That is why so many developers chose to develop for only the iPhone at the outset: It had the biggest market share and arguably offered the greatest opportunity for return on investment. Then they would turn their attention to the Android platform. As we discussed, the Android world is fragmented, with every developer on different levels of software, so developers often had to choose specific individual Android platforms to support.

These days, there are cross-platform device development tools that allow you to write once and deploy your app on different devices. You still have to comply with individual app store policies and submit your app to those stores per their specified processes. We'll get to those in a moment.

Platform Choices

Just as with the mobile web, you also need to make platform choices for mobile apps, although as the previous section indicates, it is becoming easier to support multiple platforms with a single development effort. Still, some developers choose to support either Apple or Android (the two most prominent platforms). Increasingly, app developers are supporting both, as well as Blackberry, Microsoft and others depending on target audiences and proposed use of the app. In addition, with the 2011 launch of the Kindle Fire and its reliance on the Amazon Appstore, many developers are also beginning to add Kindle Fire to the mix of supported mobile devices. Even though it is an Android-based device, it does have some different development requirements.

App Development Tools

The list of mobile web and mobile app development tools continues to grow almost daily. Here are some of the mobile app development environments available as of this writing. Once you establish specific goals and objectives for your app development projects, you can review available development environments to determine which best meet your needs. Some are very technical, IT-type environments. Others don't require a programmer to develop apps. These are listed in no particular order.

- PhoneGap is an HTML5 app platform that allows you to author native mobile apps with familiar (to programmers) HTML and JavaScript. It also gives you access to APIs (application programming interface) and app stores, so it is a fairly turnkey offering. It's why my team is using at the time of this writing. PhoneGap uses standards-based web technologies to bridge web applications and mobile devices. Since PhoneGap is an open-source implementation of open standards, developers and companies can use PhoneGap for mobile applications that are free, commercial, open source or any combination of these. PhoneGap Build is a cloud-based development service which means that you don't have to install the entire application locally. You push your app up to their machines, they build it and push it out. PhoneGap was acquired by Adobe in October of 2011 and hosts the PhoneGap online community as well as the PhoneGap Build service. Adobe contributed the PhoneGap code to the Apache Software Foundation under the name Apache Callback to ensure open stewardship of the PhoneGap project (i.e., that it will always remain free and open source under the Apache License).

- Verivo Software, formerly Pyxsis Mobile, is another option. Located in Waltham, Massachusetts, Verivo is an enterprise mobility company dedicated to helping businesses drive their mobile initiatives and improve their bottom line. The company started by designing and selling mobile apps, primarily to the financial services industry, and has evolved to directly offering its mobile platform to companies. The platform allows companies to build, deploy and manage mobility initiatives without the need to rely on outside resources to develop and run mobile apps. It is a visual development tool using a drag-and-drop development environment and configuration-based architecture that requires no programming or technical expertise. It enables the fast building and deployment of cross-device mobile applications with full native device capabilities.

- Sencha Touch is a free mobile JavaScript framework built to specifically leverage the latest standards, including HTML5, CSS3 and JavaScript to deliver components such as audio and video, as well as a local storage proxy for saving data offline. A cross-platform framework, it is compatible with Apple, Android and BlackBerry devices. It also claims to be enterprise-ready—that is, secure and robust. Apps can be developed and deployed outside the context of app stores, which means there is no need to wait for approval and acceptance in native marketplaces for apps that are enterprise-specific. It works with PhoneGap for distribution of apps to native marketplaces.

- jQueryMobile is another HTML5-based cross-platform mobile framework that allows you to design a single highly branded and customized web application that will work on all popular smartphone and tablet platforms. It also supports CSS3 for polished visuals. The jQuery Project is funded entirely by donations and contributions from the jQuery community. The jQuery Project, formed in September 2009, is part of the Software Freedom Conservancy, a non-profit dedicated to providing a home for Open Source software. The jQuery Mobile Project, design to specifically address mobile web development, was launched in August 2010.

- MotherApp is an app consultancy service that helps companies create and publish apps for the Apple App Store and Android Market. The company offers end-to-end app development and is an option if you don't want to do the development internally.

- Appcelerator Titanium is a mobile application platform that allows you to build, connect, deploy, manage and scale mobile applications for all devices and operating systems from a single platform. Titanium Studio allows the building, testing and deployment of mobile, desktop and web applications, as well as automated app packaging. The company also operates the Open Mobile Marketplace, an online marketplace for buying and selling extensions that connect Titanium apps to such things as enterprise data sources, multimedia servers and advertising and commerce solutions. It allows developers to leverage the work of others by incorporating these modules into their development efforts.

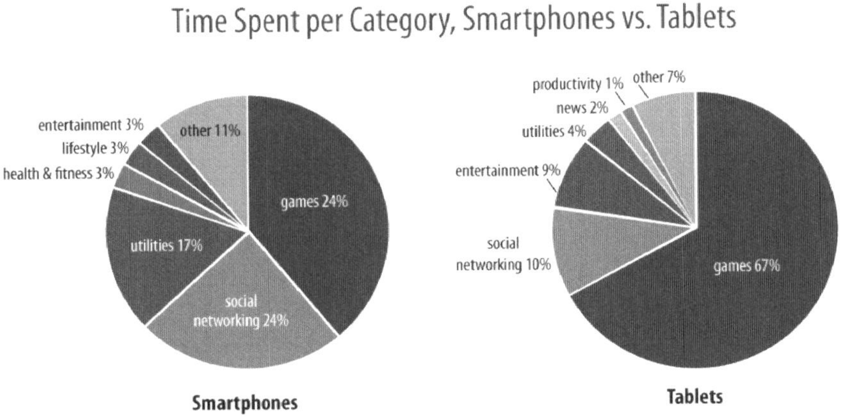

• RunRevLiveCode is an English-like language for programming apps. As of this writing, it supports iOS, but Android and Windows are "coming soon." It comes in personal or commercial versions which are priced accordingly.

•AppMakrallows you to build limited Twitter, RSS or blog feed apps for the iPhone for free. Phone support is available for a fee.

• iSites allows you to create a simple and limited app for your RSS feed, blog or other business-related social media content for iPhone and Android.

• Saasmob is a one-size-fits-all app builder that allows you to choose customized color schemes, incorporate widgets, upload a catalog or coupon and publish product news for one monthly fee.

• MobiCart allows you to build a limited mobile commerce (mcommerce) store for free. You can upload your logo, product images, set prices, and select a color theme, set up your store tabs, contact pages, news and Twitter feeds. It works in conjunction with a PayPal account.

In addition to MotherApp mentioned above, there are other services that will build your app for you, such as MyAppBuilderand Blue Toad.

Most of these examples are focused on smartphones although some have tablet components as well. It should be noted that users expect to see differences between apps developed for smartphones and those developed for tablets, taking into consideration the different functionality of the two device classes and the incremental real estate found on a tablet versus a smartphone. These differences should be taken into consideration in your development strategies. Core functionality can be developed once but the user interface and full set of features/functions should still be specialized for each of the platforms.

Two tablet-specific development apps are highlighted here:

Adobe's Digital Publishing Suite (DPS) has been available for some time in the Enterprise and Professional Editions, and is now available in the Single Edition for individual users or smaller businesses. According to Adobe, Digital Publishing Suite is a complete solution that lets individual designers, traditional media publishers, ad agencies and major media and brand organizations create, distribute, monetize and optimize interactive content and publications for tablet devices.

Digital Publishing Solution is a cloud-based model that allows users to leverage content created in Adobe InDesign into the tablet world by easily creating an iPad or other tablet app. In the case of the iPad version, once the app has been approved by the Apple App Store, it is available for download and may incur additional download fees from Adobe, as well as data storage fees. The solution also supports Android (including Kindle Fire) and Blackberry.

As one example of how DPS might be used, it is a great way for graphic designers to make their work interactive to tablets without the need to learn to write code or hire someone to do that. They can bring their creative vision all the way through to a tablet without having to hand it off to an outsider. Instead, they will be working with Adobe InDesign, a familiar tool. There are a few new things to learn about, including interactive overlays and the digital publishing tools that go with it. But overall it is an InDesign experience.

How might this be used? A design professional might be working with a local law firm, school or restaurant that wants an interactive brochure. The designer can first create the print brochure and then add interactive overlays, such as audio, video or other content for use on a tablet. For a restaurant, it might be the ability to make a reservation or view their wine selection, including the ability to get detailed information about the winery. For a law firm, perhaps a video of one of the partners speaking about a practice area they specialize in can be included in an interactive brochure made available to key clients and prospects. The opportunities are limited only by the creativity of the designer and the content owner.

The app could be used in a variety of ways. For example, one upscale restaurant in Atlanta hands iPads to clients who want more detail about its extensive wine list. In the pharmaceutical industry, sales people can use customized apps to conduct a more engaging conversation with physicians. In other cases, the potential customer might download a useful app for free. The University of Dayton used Single Edition to produce its annual brochure for incoming freshmen, with an interactive magazine about the school, the town, the sports and social scene and academics. In another example, a 10-person firm that designs and builds homes added floor plans, the ability to get a 360-degree view of the house by rotating the elevation of the house and more to the interactive version of its brochure.

Twixl Media, located in Belgium, offers Twixl Publisher, licensed software installed internally on the user's computer or server as opposed to Adobe's cloud-based model. It allows more independence in app builds and allows users to host their own content, thereby avoiding hosting or download fees. Twixl's license includes maintenance for the first year, and users have the option of renewing maintenance in subsequent years, or not. Without maintenance, they can continue to use the software but will not receive upgrades.

Twixl Publisher is comprised of an InDesign Plug-In, the Builder app, and a reader app. To create an iPad app, the user exports an InDesign file to Twixl's Builder app, which creates an iPad reader app that can be displayed in the iPad simulator on the Mac. Once the app has been approved by the designer and content owner, it can be installed either through iTunes, outside the Apple App Store or, if the user wants to utilize the App Store (depending on the type of license), either Twixl Media will create the App Store build or the user can create it using the advanced version.

Twixl Publisher 2.0 is available with four licensing options:

- ***Twixl Publisher Explore***: this entry-level version is available as a free download, and allows you to create iPad app previews and ad hoc builds that can be distributed in house. There is a per-build "pay-as-you-go" option for App Store builds.
- ***Twixl Publisher Premium***: a single user version that lets you independently create an unlimited number of ad hoc or App Store builds. It is ideal for individual designers and smaller shops that regularly want to create branded App Store apps.
- ***Twixl Publisher Advanced***: a 5-user workgroup version that lets you independently create an unlimited number of ad hoc, App Store and Enterprise builds, and use Google Analytics. It is ideal for workgroups and for companies wanting to distribute in house content via Apple's iOS Developer Enterprise program.
- ***Twixl Publisher Professional***: offers all features of the advanced version, and in addition allows you to create storefront or kiosk apps with support for in-app purchase and subscriptions. It is targeted towards magazine publishers.

As of this writing, Twixl Media is also developing an Android version of Twixl Publisher.

Getting the Word Out

Now that you have developed your own app(s), how do you get the word out? With the hundreds of thousands of apps out there across seven major app stores, it is a crowded playing field. But do not despair. For an untethered and knowledgeable individual, there are many ways to get the word out to your target audience. Whether your app is free or paid, its success will depend on how useful or attractive it is to your target market. If it doesn't add value for the user, there is no point in developing it.

Assuming there is unique and compelling value-add, the next challenge is marketing your app(s). This is an area where you can't really rely on traditional marketing techniques. Traditional marketing, such as banner ads, pay-per-click campaigns and even TV, radio and print advertising, targets the mass market. And while there are lots of smartphones out there, not everyone has one! Using these traditional vehicles can mean excessively high user acquisition costs. It is more appropriate to use mobile-specific advertising. These include:

- Mobile ad networks that display your ads via their network of mobile publishers
- Real-time bidding platforms that allow you to bid on mobile traffic
- Incentive-based download programs, where users are incentivized to download your app.

Of course, you can also promote your app to current customers and targeted prospects through direct marketing, including direct mail, email, PR campaigns, social media, and even QR codes. Your web site is also a valuable channel for promoting your app(s).

In addition, since the world of mobile apps is dynamic, to say the least, it is important to constantly track how your app is doing and adjust your marketing strategies—and app functionality—accordingly.

There are a number of tools available that allow you to track your app's performance. These include:

- Brightcove
- Fiksu
- Compuware

- Bango
- Piwik
- Flurry
- Mtiks
- AppClix
- Localytics

You can gain details about app performance including performance in specific date ranges, total installs, total sessions (a session begins when your app is opened and ends when it is closed), total usage time and average session length.

This tracking capability is important, not only to enable you to measure your success in terms of downloads, but also to monitor what happens next. Remember that for every four apps that are downloaded, one is never used again, and you don't want yours to fall into that sad category! If you are not tracking how users interact with your app and using that information to profile high-value users, you are missing a marketing opportunity. Depending upon the purpose of your app, you should identify the most important post-download events (Is it in-app purchases? Number of price comparisons sought? Or in the case of the home builder, number of floor plans reviewed and total time spent with the app?) Each app will have different success metrics. Be sure to define and measure yours.

Is There an App in Your Future?

The answer is likely yes. You should certainly take the time to consider how mobile apps can be part of your untethered marketing strategy. Talk to customers, brainstorm with your team, keep in touch with the latest developments in mobile apps … and dip your toes into the mobile app waters. You will be glad that you did. Scan the QR Code to download the *"Laser Beam"* QR Code scanner app for your smartphone.

Chapter Five: The Untethered Business

As you can see from our discussions so far, the relationships between businesses and their customers/prospects are rapidly changing. Not only do we have the issue of who has more control (the answer is the customers - clearly), but we also have changes in the way information is sought, transmitted, received and acted upon. Businesses today must stay in tune with these dynamics. Their strategies, tactics and yes, even the way they are organized and operate, must change if they are going to remain competitive and profitable.

Although we have focused heavily on retail with respect to how mobile marketing and communications are being used, the changes are much broader than that. Retail is bearing the first brunt of (or benefiting first from) the mobile wave, and there are lots of good examples there. But in the end, this transformation will affect the way all businesses interact with customers and prospects, as well as how they operate internally.

In Chapter Two, we saw how leveraging cloud computing can remove a great deal of infrastructure from the corporate HQ, in terms of staffing, hardware, space and cost, as well as making corporate applications more accessible to workers on the move. In Chapters Three and Four, we saw how mobile communications are making it easier for individuals to perform an ever-increasing array of actions and functionality from anywhere they happen to be.

These trends are changing the relationships between businesses and their customers. There is no question about that. But the underlying technologies we have been discussing also present significant opportunities for change in the way companies are organized and operate. These technologies are already affecting the way people work, and the relationships between employees and employers.

The Virtual (Untethered) Organization

Way back in 1993, William Davidow, a venture capitalist, and Michael Malone, a business writer, foresaw what they called the "virtual corporation," bringing together findings on the effectson companies of information technologies, organizational dynamics and manufacturing systems. Their book, *The Virtual Corporation*, highlighted some very early adopters of the virtual strategy, including Lenscrafters and Taco Bell Express. They explained how ad hoc aggregates of companies, or virtual corporations were combining to deliver instantaneous, customized services and products, and defining new linkages between company, supplier and consumer.

These visionaries were way ahead of their time. Two decades later, their predictions certainly ring true. What they called the virtual corporation, we are calling untethered businesses. Although they foresaw many things, even these bright guys couldn't possibly have foreseen the impact cloud computing and mobile communications have had in the last couple of years—and will continue to have—on businesses and their customers in 2013 and beyond. But their basic concepts were solid. If you can lay your hands on a copy of this out-of-print book, it would be worth your while to give it a read. (Amazon has some used copies!)

So what is an untethered—or virtual—business? Les Pang, Ph.D., of ISACA,[54] describes a virtual organization as, "A flexible network of independent entities linked by information technology to share skills, knowledge and access to others' expertise in nontraditional ways," saying, "Virtual organizations do not need to have all of the people, or sometimes any of the people, in one place to deliver their service. The organization exists but you cannot see it. It is a network, not an office."

In a paper submitted to the *Journal of Computer-Mediated Communication*, Scott M. Preston from Michigan State University, had this to say about virtual (read: untethered) organizations: "Virtual organization requires a different way of perceiving the world by

---

[54]A nonprofit, independent membership association, ISACA is a leading global provider of knowledge, certifications, community, advocacy and education on information systems assurance, control and security, enterprise governance of IT, and IT-related risk and compliance. Founded in 1969 as the EDP Auditors Association, ISACA helps its members and their employers ensure trust in, and value from, information systems.

those who wish to participate in it. There are four key characteristics of virtual organization as process. First, virtual organization entails the development of relationships with a broad range of potential partners, each having a particular competency that complements the others. Second, virtual organizing capitalizes on the mobility and responsiveness of telecommunications to overcome problems of distance. Third, timing is a key aspect of relationships, with actors using responsiveness and availability to decide between alternatives. Last, there must be trust between actors separated in space for virtual organization to be effective."

Trust is Key to Untethered Success

Do You Have Remote or Mobile Workers?

These can be folks who are working from home or from a remote office you may have set up, such as a sales office, or they may be workers who are on the road a great deal of time. They may even be employees who do come to the office, but also work from home on one or more days per week. These types of arrangements are becoming increasingly common and have lots of advantages if management can get past the trust issues.

One thing we do to support this mobile lifestyle is provide everyone who comes to work for our company with a smartphone. People are often surprised when they hear this, especially other executives. They say it costs too much. Not really. The value is almost immediately paid back by the advantages this approach gives my employees and my company.

Do you have any idea how much value I get when someone answers their phone at 8:00 at night, whether it is a customer problem or some other issue such as a server problem? It means we can address issues in real time, before they become catastrophic. In fact, we can deal with issues before they even become problems in the first place. Having the smartphone lets our people see inquiries in real time; things like customers signing up for a webinar, sales leads coming in, people signing up for newsletters, customers asking for help—most people can't do that. I certainly don't expect my staff to be on duty 24/7, and I do expect them to work at having a good work/life balance. But I do have an exceptionally dedicated staff who can use mobile resources to continue performing at peak levels. The smartphone comes with no strings attached. My employees can do whatever they want with it. But it allows them to be physically untethered from the office and still do a better job for us because of the real-time nature of the communications a smartphone allows.

We have also just recently given the entire management team iPads as a pilot. If things go well and we see value to the program, every employee will get an iPad. Sure, it costs $500 or more, depending on the configuration. But it gives them the tools that allow them to connect. Of course, just as with the smartphone, they can use it for other things. To me, it is a complete no-brainer. This is also a great way to enhance employee loyalty.

There are some real above-and-beyond stories this program has generated. We had a large account with a big problem, and their account manager was handling it from the hospital emergency room. The customer still talks about that one—talk about going above and beyond. I don't encourage that, of course. I want my team to take care of themselves and their families first. But the bottom line is that this created an unbelievable customer service experience for that customer. And it was enabled because we give our employees the tools to connect to the office from wherever and whenever they are.

Another great story involved an IT issue. Adam Meixler was in a field in Maine, in the middle of nowhere, waiting for his turn to go skydiving (he had the day off). Some data accidentally got overwritten in one of our systems, and we urgently needed to get it back. Adam used an iPad app called iTap that allows remote desktop access via phone or iPad communication (described in Chapter Four). He was able to use his iPad with 3G connectivity, restore the data, and then take his turn jumping out of a plane. This meant we didn't need to wait until the next day to fix the problem, Adam could enjoy the vast majority of his day off, and we were back up and running in a few minutes.

Let's face it, today's workforce and today's students (tomorrow's workforce) are truly the "ME" generation. For them, it is all about "ME." For them, the flexibility of working from anywhere is expected, and they don't have a problem working from home. It is an old way of thinking to say that employees must be in the office to get work done. Of course, there are times when it is required. That is to be expected. But giving people the flexibility to work from wherever they are, and the tools to do so, is absolutely critical to an untethered business. It's the core of it.

Some people are more productive at home, some at the office, some at other locations. Employees should be given the option to work from wherever is most productive for them, within the constraints of organizational needs.

Who Are These Mobile Workers?

According to IDC's broad definition of mobile workers, three-quarters of the work force in North America were mobile in 2010, surpassing an earlier forecast that projected reaching that level by 2013.[55] The research firm indicates that the Americas region, which includes the United States, Canada, and Latin America, will see the number of mobile workers grow from 182.5 million in 2010 to 212.1 million in 2015.

IDC broadly segments the mobile worker population into three core categories: office-based mobile workers, non-office-based mobile workers, and home-based mobile workers.[56] "Wait," you might say, "how can an office-based worker be a mobile worker? The others I can understand." IDC defines these as mobile professionals that are away from their primary workplace 20% or more of the time, such as traveling executives (like me!), sales reps, insurance agents, pharmaceutical reps, etc. Others within this category include those that are mobile less than 20% of their workdays per month, or are mobile within the office or campus environment, such as IT professionals traveling within buildings or campuses. IDC also includes mobile on-location workers such as warehouse or hospitality workers.

---

[55] *Worldwide Mobile Worker Population 2011-2015 Forecast, IDC*, December 2011.
[56] *Worldwide Mobile Worker Population 2011-2015 Forecast, IDC*, December 2011.

Within these groups of mobile workers, those who present the biggest challenge for many companies are non-office-based and home-based workers. If you can't see them, how do you know they are working? Companies with distributed sales and service forces have been dealing with this for a long time, and many have intensive reporting processes in place to monitor them—if not daily activities, then certainly some sort of results-based monitoring, such as the number of customer calls or performance against sales plans. For other types of workers, it can be more difficult to establish and monitor appropriate metrics. This is why it is important to have clear and concise job descriptions in place, as well as individual measurable goals and objectives for each employee that are periodically reviewed to ensure that employees—regardless of where they are located—are performing as expected. Managers must shift the emphasis from transactional, day-to-day performance of tasks by their employees to a focus on results and deliverables. This can be a difficult transition for many managers, but it is an essential one. Not only will the employees be happier with less micromanagement, but managers will be freed up to take on more strategic activities. Everyone wins in this scenario.

Geography Becomes an Un-Barrier in an Untethered World

One significant advantage of an untethered business: You don't need to rely on resources in a single geographic area. This allows you to source the best person for the job regardless of where they live. Sure, some jobs will need to remain in the corporate location (if you choose to keep one!). But there are likely fewer of those jobs than you might think.

For example, consider how easy it is to conduct a video call. It's still free on Skype! For as little as $50 per month, you can subscribe to GoToMeeting, which allows you to share not only video, but desktops and all of their contents. You can also do webinars for larger groups from anywhere using inexpensive solutions such as GoToWebinar. Cloud-based Google Apps allows multiple people to simultaneously view and edit the same document (or spreadsheet or presentation) while on a video or standard telephone conference call. Basecamp is a project management tool specifically designed for untethered workgroups. Everyone on a project can see exactly what needs to be done when, assign and track action items, and whiteboard ideas and brainstorms for sharing with the entire team. These tools, and others like them, make a collaborative work process easy, regardless of where the parties are located.

Think about it. Does it make sense to spend thousands of dollars relocating a new employee to your corporate headquarters, not to mention having them uproot their families? Despite the economic situation (or perhaps because of it) fewer prospective employees are willing to relocate for a new job. Families are entrenched, kids are in school, spouses are employed … there are many reasons for an employee not wanting to move, not the least of which is the potential insecurity of a long-term arrangement with the new company. Management teams change, companies come and go, and many other things can happen that can make such a move difficult to swallow. This means that you, the employer, have restricted the base of qualified people from which you can choose to put together that All-Star team.

What about meetings, you ask? Don't you need people in a room together to make them effective? The answer is 'yes'. Sometimes. And that's what airplanes are for. But as you try out some of the collaborative tools that are available today—such as Skype, Google Apps, Basecamp and GoToMeeting—you are likely to find that the meetings that require someone to hop on a plane are fewer and farther between than you might imagine.

Even servers can be managed remotely, whether they are in the cloud or in your server room. Even from a field in Maine in the middle of nowhere! Sure, someone might need to reboot a computer or do some other type of physical maintenance on it, but that person could be a less skilled individual acting under the direction of an IT guru who is miles away, perhaps showing them what to do using Skype video calling.

I recently heard a story about a young man, a programmer, who emigrated from Poland to the U.S. Upon arriving in New York City, he hopped on a bus with a plan to see the Great United States. When he got to South Dakota, he decided to stay a while, and secured a job as a caretaker of someone's home. There he met a girl, fell in love, got married and decided to stay. All this time, he was still working for the same Polish company, programming—midnight to 8 AM! Wishing to find a local job, he heard about a direct marketing company in the area that was hiring and drove to their building. Using their free WiFi network, he sat in the parking lot, perused their web site, created several new web pages, printed them out, and walked in to apply for the job—which he got! Is he still programming for the Polish company at night? Probably. But the owner of the direct marketing company is thrilled with this employee and the results he has brought to the company. He was impressed by his innovative thinking and proactive approach to the job. Sure, in this case, he is working at corporate headquarters, but more than likely he could just as easily work remotely, as he had been doing for the Polish firm for some time.

The Benefits of Mobility

Once you get used to the idea, having employees work from a remote location can offer many benefits. It can mean a better quality of life for the employee. It's better for the environment—it takes wasteful commutes out of the equation. An hour commute each way, which is not unusual these days, means 10 wasted hours per week (and all that expensive fuel!). That's a lot of time and gas! That's time and gas that could be put to more productive use. You require less office space and infrastructure, saving money. You can source qualified employees from a wider geographic range.

Not everyone is suited to working remotely, and not every job can be performed that way. Some people need the social interaction that comes from going to an office every day. Others don't work well in an unstructured environment. But for an increasing number, a remote work style suits them; they often can be more efficient and productive than they would be in an office, where there are likely to be more interruptions. And as more Millennials come into the work force, it is likely that this trend will continue to grow. Millennials or not, today's employees increasingly expect—and are more motivated in—a flexible mobile working environment than in a traditional one. Even for those who need—or think they need—frequent in-person social interaction, using social media, instant messaging and collaborative technologies can often offset that need—sort of a virtual water cooler—making those employees more comfortable with their remote status.

An iPass study[57] also pointed out another advantage: making use of dead time. Especially with deadlines looming, dead time associated with taking care of important matters - such as a worker seeking medical attention for himself or a child, or waiting for a delayed flight (or even during a flight, since more and more are equipped with WiFi) - can be aggravating and frustrating. The study indicated that 83% of respondents use mobile technologies to make use of this dead time at least occasionally. Sometimes this even allows them to finish work that might otherwise need to be done late at night in a hotel room, or when they return home.

I can personally attest to the efficiency of this model. I travel a lot and have my share of delayed flights, wait time between appointments or before giving a speech, and even driving (well, riding with someone) to client meetings. I make the most of this dead time—and I do—with my personal arsenal of mobile technologies. And that means that my mind is able to fully focus on my family when I return home, or attend the hockey games my sons are playing. In the end, even though I feel like I am "always on," I also feel that my quality of life has significantly improved due to the added flexibility mobile technologies have brought into my lifestyle. And I am not alone in feeling this way. The danger is never turning it off. There is a delicate balance that must be achieved. I don't want my kids looking back and saying, "Gee, my dad was working all the time, even when he was pretending to watch me play hockey." So I work very hard at seeing that that does not happen. And I set that example for my staff as well.

---

[57]Source: *The Well-being of the Mobile Workforce*, by Dr. Carolyn Axtell, Institute of Work Psychology, the Management School, University of Sheffield, UK. Source:

Mobile Workforce Becoming Mainstream

Whether or not your company has embraced a mobile workforce, the majority have. According to a study conducted by the Telework Coalition:

- 89 of the top 100 U.S. companies offer telecommuting;
- 58 percent of companies consider themselves a virtual workplace;
- Only nine percent of employees worked at headquarters; and
- 67 percent of all workers used mobile and wireless computing.[58]

The point is, an untethered strategy applies to how you deal with customers, but it also applies to how you deal with employees or contractors—or even business partners. Take what you have learned about cloud computing and mobile communications, take a serious look at how your company is organized, and be creative about how you structure your organization. Implementing an untethered—or virtual—strategy may be just the ticket for taking your company to the next level. You'll never know unless you try.

10 Tips for Managing a Mobile Workforce

And when you do try, keep in mind these suggestions for managing a mobile workforce, compliments of National Association of Women Business Owners (NAWBO) and makingstories.net:[59]

1. Focus on building relationships - It's that trust thing. You must be able to trust your mobile workers, and they must be able to trust you. Without that trust, and without strong relationships, managing a dispersed team of mobile workers can be extremely difficult.

2. Streamline communications. Try some of the tools we have mentioned here—Skype, GoToMeeting, GoogleApps, iTap. Don't forget instant messaging. Put a communications plan in

---

[58]Source: *The Mobile Workforce and Enterprise Applications: 2007-2012*, The Insight Research Corporation

[59]*The Top Ten Strategies for Mangers of Mobile Workers: Surviving and Thriving in the Emerging Mobile Workforc*e, by Terrence L. Gargiulo, President, makingstories.net

place to make sure your entire team stays on the same page, understands the priorities, stays in touch and is set to produce expected deliverables in a timely fashion.

3. Incorporate less didactic forms of communications. This means that the office memo as the primary means of communication is out in most cases. The key is to have an inclusive communications strategy in place that makes team members feel a part of the team and gets the right level of information out there so they can effectively accomplish their work. One thing we do, as I have already mentioned, is hold an all-hands meeting one Friday per month. We order lunch in (at our expense), and I use that time to review business (I want everyone to know exactly how we are doing so they can do their best to make sure we do even better!); recognize employees, either for exceptional performance or birthdays and other special events (we give folks a really nice personalized gift when they reach their five-year anniversary); allow the team to ask questions. Sometimes we have special guests at these meetings who can contribute industry knowledge or other important developmental information. Remote or mobile employees tune in via phone or video if possible, so everyone truly feels like part of a team.

4. Spend more time listening. This is a good piece of lifestyle advice, period. But it is really important when working with a distributed team. Making listening a priority may be the single most important thing you do in managing mobile workers. In addition to our monthly meetings, where all kinds of questions are asked, I have an open door (or open phone) policy. Everyone knows they can come to me with anything, and there will be no negative ramifications, regardless of what it is.

5. Let mobile workers define communication and reporting practices they want to follow. This is not counterintuitive to having a communications plan in place. It is part of empowering workers to do their jobs in creative and

innovative ways. It is part of building trust and relationships. It does not mean, however, that anyone is off the hook in terms of delivering against expectations. If you run into issues in this regard, you may need to pull back on this one a bit as you work through issues with individual employees.

6. Manage deliverables not activities. As we said earlier, this can be one of the most difficult transitions for a manager to make. But it is an important one. The deliverables are the most important part of the job. How, when and where these deliverables are produced is less important, as long as they meet requirements, including timeliness and completeness. Remember, micromanaging is counterproductive, for you and for them.

7. Engage in more frequent and informal performance management activities. That mandatory annual performance review will probably always be there. But keeping in frequent touch with mobile workers relative to their performance goals and personal development plans is a critical element of building that relationship of trust. Tip No. 4 is important here, too. Be sure to spend more time listening than talking! These are significant inclusive activities that can help you ensure you have a cohesive team as well as aid in the prevention of problems/issues before they develop into something major.

8. Give complete trust until given a concrete behavioral reason to do otherwise. Back to listening and trust again. But when trust has been violated, you must take action.

9. Use adaptive management styles tailored to individual workers. Every employee is different and each requires a slightly different management style, based on their knowledge, experience, tenure, performance and maturity. Be sure to take a personalized approach to managing individual team members.

10. Leverage technology. Don't be the one jumping on planes to make the rounds of your mobile workers! That defeats the whole purpose. Not that you should never do that, of course, but use travel judiciously. We've already highlighted some of the technologies that allow you to "almost be there" and to manage these mobile teams effectively. Use them.

The Dark Side of Mobility

And there is one more I would like to add to this very thorough list: Make sure your mobile workers are equipped with the right technology! Do they have a quiet place in which to work in their home, if they are working from home? If not, explore other alternatives for them. What about furniture? Make sure they can work comfortably, especially if they spend any significant amount of time working at a computer. These days, bandwidth shouldn't be an issue, but make sure your mobile team has plenty of it. With some 70% of American homes having Internet connectivity, and with numerous, and often free, WiFi locations outside the home, your mobile team is likely to have sufficient connectivity. But don't assume. Make sure they have what they need, and keep their computers, tablets and phones updated, too!

The dark side of mobility, as we have already mentioned, is its always-on nature. This can have a negative effect on the health and welfare of employees, and executives and managers should be aware of these pitfalls. In addition to making sure employees have a reasonable and well-equipped place to work when they are not in the office, it is also important to encourage employees to take care of their health, getting sufficient sleep, eating right and taking the time to exercise.

According to the iPass Global Workforce Report,[60] mobile workers tend to put in more hours per year—an average of 240 hours more. One in four mobile workers reported sleeping less than six hours per night, attributing this loss of sleep to the demands of work. Most studies indicate that the average adult needs seven to nine hours

---

[60] *The iPass Global Mobile Workforce Report: Understanding Enterprise Mobility Trends and Mobile Usage*, 4Q2011

of sleep per night. In addition, travel and work commitments are eating into exercise time as well. The iPass study reflected that 56% of respondents are exercising erratically or not at all. Both of these factors—lack of sleep and exercise—ultimately affect the employee's well-being, ability to perform and overall productivity. With enough sleep and adequate exercise, minds are sharper and employees are more effective. It pays to take the time to take care of these health-related activities. Employers should encourage their staff to do so.

Vacations are another important health factor. Employees should be encouraged to take that time off, disconnecting as much as possible in order to unwind and relax. They will return to work in a much better frame of mind. The good news is, according to the iPass study, 63% of North American workers are taking all of their vacation time, although 21% reported taking less than half. Make sure your folks are not in that 21%.

Corporate Mobility: What Does It Mean for IT?

This transition to an untethered business will definitely impact the IT organization. We have already discussed some of the ways in which cloud computing is changing the level of involvement IT must have in many enterprise applications. But what about mobile devices?

Corporate IT departments have historically tried very hard to control the devices that can access their corporate networks, and for good reason. But times are continuing to change from out underneath IT departments' feet. Company-purchased and administered laptops, BlackBerrys issued by the company and mandated as the smartphone standard—these approaches are rapidly going by the wayside.

Security, of course, was one huge concern that drove these policies. But IT support (help desk) was another. It was simply too expensive to have staff available to support too many different platforms. But all of that is changing. The iPass survey referenced earlier reports that when facing technical issues, 81% of respondents contacted IT as a last resort, while only 2% had IT on speed dial. Mobile workers seem to be a more technically savvy lot, and the days of troubleshooting a user's PC that isn't working because it isn't plugged in are probably at an end.

The other trend is less control over which devices can access corporate networks. Rather than specifying a specific device that must be used (such as a BlackBerry), companies are either providing lists from which employees can choose, or allowing them to use the device of their choice (only 28% of mobile workers were given no choice, according to iPass). Along with this comes a shift in who owns the devices. Increasingly, individuals will own those devices, whether they are smartphones or tablets, although companies will continue to provide support for Android- and Apple-based devices, and, of course, monitor them from a security perspective. And in 2012 and beyond, tablets will increasingly make their way into the enterprise, either as employee-owned devices, or as business tools that include custom apps designed to further the goals and objectives of the enterprise.

These trends do not eliminate the need for an IT department by any means. But they do mean that IT departments can leverage such tools as self-service portals, discussion boards and wikis that allow users to support each other for the less knotty problems, and turn their expertise to addressing more difficult issues that will deliver more value to the organization and make better use of their skills and talents.

As you make the transition to an untethered business, these are considerations you should keep in mind.

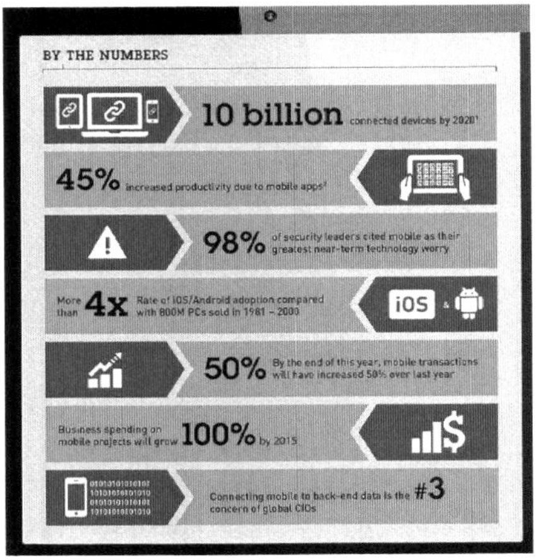

Source: *rcrwireless.com*

Chapter Six: Social Media: Where Does It Fit?

There is no way I could write this book without devoting a chapter to Social Media. It is clearly a huge element of the untethered business and untethered marketing practices. Consider this: Facebook is the most downloaded Android app, and number two over all considering all of the app stores. According to PaidContent,[61] as shown in the chart below, as of December 27, 2011, there were more than 300 million monthly active users of Facebook's' mobile apps. That is 37.5% of the 800 million total monthly active users of Facebook (up to 845 million by Facebook's initial IPO filing in early 2012). According to PaidContent, 70% of mobile users, and 30% of all users, used apps to access Facebook. And that's just the leading example of the merging of social media and mobile communications. There are many more, of course, not the least of which is Twitter.

Figure 5. Active Users of Facebook Apps (m), 27 Dec 2011

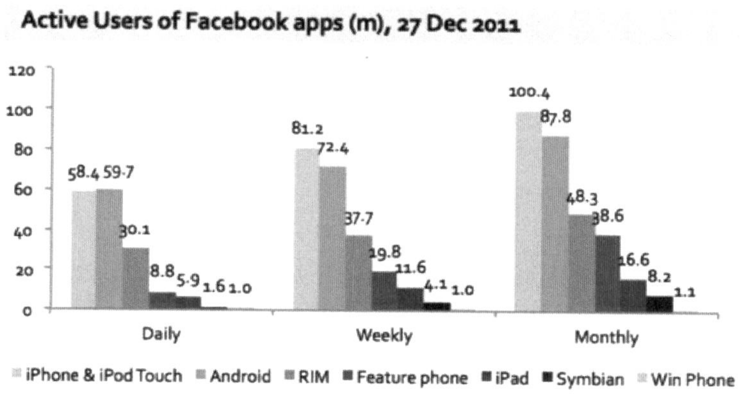

[Source: Facebook, Enders Analysis]

This chapter is a social media primer, of sorts. It will contain the most up-to-date information about the most popular social media platforms, including number of users; how these platforms are used, both by

[61] Almost 40 Percent of Fac

businesses and consumers; tips for leveraging them for business; and much more. We will also discuss how to measure your social media score (how do you rank in the world of social media, both personally and as a business), and why that is important. All of this is important foundation for Chapter Seven, where we will be discussing how to build an untethered marketing plan, the real core of this book.

Because anything written about social media is obsolete almost before the ink is dry on the paper (or the pixels are displayed on the screen!), please be sure to check out our special resource site (newpathtoprofit.com) for this book which we will keep updated as new trends and data emerge.

Let's start with the basics about key social media sites. But before we do: Full disclosure - I own an online marketing company, Grow Socially, which helps service providers in their efforts to include social media in their marketing and services mix. The book is not a sales pitch for this business, but I thought you should know.

Social Media: A Market Reality

Social media is not a gimmick or a fad. It is here to stay, although its face changes almost daily. It is a new way of communicating using highly accessible and scalable publishing technologies. Social media is designed to make it easy to create and disseminate user-created content, and in fact, transform users from content consumers (think broadcast television or printed publications) to content creators.

We are still in the early stages of the evolution of social media (despite the fact that Facebook has 845 million members worldwide!). So there are no firm and fixed guidelines such as those you might find in older, more established media. There are, however, certain unwritten rules of social media etiquette that we will explore later in this chapter.

I like to think of social media as a part of the online marketing channel, and the components you use—Facebook, Twitter, LinkedIn or others—are tactics. It all starts with a plan. That's right: Strategy before tactics. In Chapter Seven, we will talk more about the overall untethered marketing plan. In this chapter, strategy and tactics discussed are specific to social media, a subset of the whole.

Many large companies have a strong social media presence. For example, as of this writing, more than 39 million people "Like" Coca-Cola on Facebook, and 750 thousand are talking about Coke there. The Coca-Cola Facebook Page, according to its House Rules, is intended to provide a place for fans of Coca-Cola to discuss the company's beverages and promotions. In this case, the company has established guidelines for users wishing to post content, which includes a disclaimer that content posted to the page does not represent the opinions of The Coca-Cola Company, and the company retains the right to remove objectionable material.

But imagine: Coca-Cola has ready access to more than 39 million of its customers! And more than 750 thousand of them are carrying on a conversation about the company and its products! The company can peruse the comments, images and other content that has been posted, get insight into how consumers feel about its products, and even solicit input about new product plans or recently launched products or planned events. It's like a giant focus group, only it doesn't require going into those drab mall conference rooms with 10 people sitting around a table and who knows how many watching from behind the mirrored glass.

That being said, marketers are still struggling a bit with how to monetize their social media presence. It does require an investment—in the case of Coca-Cola, there is likely at least one full-time person behind the scenes monitoring posts to the Coca-Cola page. I counted 30 posts in just one hour on one morning while this book was in progress—from all around the world and in different languages. So while it might not be directly driving revenue, there is an intrinsic value to having this wealth of consumer feedback to guide the company in its future product development, advertising and other strategies, and to build increased customer loyalty by keeping the dialog going. Perhaps how to monetize your social media presence is the wrong question to be asking. Rather, it should be considered as part of the overall communications strategy of any successful company today.

Social Media gives customers the opportunity to engage with brands in a more intimate way than ever before. They can share praise, post questions, and complain. No matter what they are doing, brands can receive benefits. Having a place where consumers can go to express their opinions—good or bad—is invaluable. And if the brand owner is responsive to these opinions and comments, all the better.

Social media is one of the best ways to get noticed online and to build relationships. Social media sites help to further your brand, increase visibility, encourage web site traffic, improve customer service and more.

Figure 6. Content Distribution Strategy

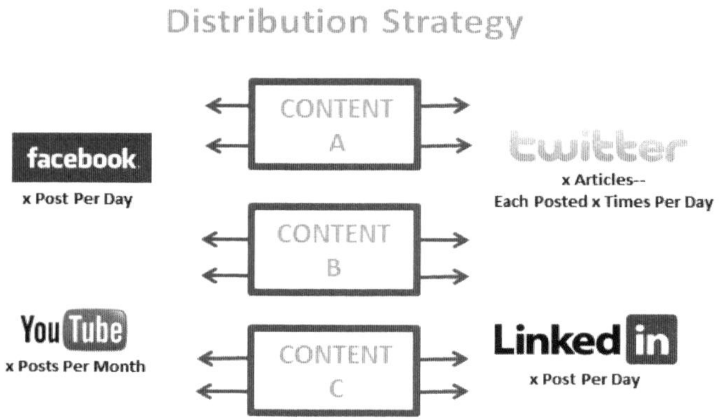

Figure 6 helps demonstrate how you should view your social media channels in relation to your website – the promotion should work both ways.

How can you use social media as part of your marketing strategy?

- Brand promotion
- Building buzz
- Customer / prospect interaction
- Tracking your online reputation

Why is branding important in social media? My answer is: "It is your brand! Protect it and use it!" From the name you acquire as your Twitter username right down to the graphics you use on your social media pages, you must view these types of decisions as important and as items that can enhance or detract from your brand.

But there are so many social media sites out there that it can be confusing. Which sites should you build your profile on? On how many sites should you create a presence? And how are you going to keep up with it all?

The number one tip I can offer is to have an online marketing plan. This is a subset of your overall marketing plan—your new "untethered" marketing plan (see Chapter Seven). Your plan will incorporate your strategy for deploying and measuring the tactics you will use online.

Top Social Media Sites for Marketers

The danger of creating profiles on more than a handful of social media sites is that you spread yourself too thin. You end up failing to create any buzz or relating to any prospects on any of the sites. So it is important to start with a small number of sites where you can easily maintain a presence.

One thing to keep in mind is that everything you do on these social media sites is online and public, and is basically there forever. So keeping everything on a professional level is critical. You can certainly have fun with it, but you don't want to do anything to damage your business reputation. That is why companies like Coca-Cola invest significant efforts in monitoring sites like Facebook and removing objectionable content that doesn't comply with its House Rules. That doesn't mean censorship or removing anything the company doesn't like. For example, in the debate about whether Coca-Cola should be using sugar instead of high fructose corn syrup, one user posted an opinion that Pepsi was better. That was not removed, nor should it have been. In social media, you do not want to censor, but as your communities grow, you may find it beneficial to publish rules as Coke did, and then manage the site according to those rules.

So…where should you concentrate your social media efforts? There are three top social media sites that are most likely to benefit your untethered marketing efforts—Twitter, Facebook and LinkedIn. And coming up fast is Google+ (Google Plus). First, let's describe what each of these sites is, and then I will provide a complete guide for using each of them. As you get more familiar with the social media universe, and as new sites start gaining traction (such as Google+), you may choose to add others to the mix. But these three are a good place to start.

Twitter

Wikipedia describes Twitter, created in 2006, as a free social networking and microblogging service that enables its users to send and read messages known as tweets. Tweets are text-based posts of up to 140 characters (including spaces) displayed on the author's profile page and delivered to the author's subscribers who are known as followers. Senders can restrict delivery to those in their circle of friends or, by default, allow open access. Ever since late 2009, users can follow lists of authors instead of following individual authors. All users can send and receive tweets via the Twitter website, Short Message Service (SMS) or external applications. While the service itself costs nothing to use, accessing it through SMS may incur phone service provider fees.

Although historically Twitter closely guarded its usage statistics, the company has become more open about volumes. In October of 2011, Twitter CEO Dick Costolo revealed that Twitter users were sending 250 million tweets per day, compared to 2 million per day in January of 2009 and 65 million per day in mid-2010.According to Costolo, Twitter has over 100 million global active users, half of those logging in every day. Mobile usage is growing by 40% each quarter.

Even so, Twitter remains just a fraction of the size of Facebook in terms of number of users (discussed next).Facebook counts more than 850 million active users, more than half of which the company claims log in at least once daily. Twitter's Costolo stated that his goal is to keep Twitter's offering simple, and he believes that sets it apart from Facebook.

Tweets can be promotional in nature, informational, fun or entertaining—and should include a mix of these. Simply using it as a promotional tool will not be well-accepted by your community and could cause people to "unfollow" you as well as recommend the same to their friends. Ideally, your tweets should be "re-tweetable." This means that other Twitter users find your content worthy of repeating to their group of followers. In this way, good content can actually go viral as it spreads from network to network. While Twitter may appear to be a one-way conversation, it is anything but. You should be conversing and building relationships with others using this medium. Some of the options you have with Twitter are retweeting, replying to tweets and sending direct (personal) messages to other Twitter users. Many companies use Twitter as part of their customer service/support strategy as well as in marketing efforts. This is where direct messaging can come in handy, allowing real-time discussion of customer issues in a private conversation.

Facebook

According to Wikipedia,[62] Facebook, founded in February of 2004 from a Harvard University dorm room, is a social networking website that is operated and privately owned by Facebook, Inc. as of this writing. However, Facebook filed a much-awaited and historic IPO on February 1, 2012, that could potentially dwarf rival Google's record 2004 IPO. It could value the company at as much as $100 billion and raise as much as $10 billion (Google's IPO raised $1.9 billion with a valuation of $23 billion). It was the first public reveal of Facebook's financial status. In its filing, the company reported $3.71 billion in revenues and $1 billion in profits in 2011. Eighty-five percent of revenues came from advertising; the balance came from social gaming and other fees.

Facebook users can add friends, send them messages, and update their personal profiles to notify friends about themselves. Additionally, users can join networks organized by city, workplace, and school or

[62] Information and statistics about various social media venues cited in this document come from Wikipedia and other online sources (including published company data) as of February 2010

college. The website's name stems from the colloquial name of books given at the start of the academic year by university administrations with the intention of helping students to get to know each other better. While Facebook may have started as a college/university phenomenon, the majority of Facebook users today are outside of colleges and universities.

Facebook has fielded many concerns about privacy issues, but continues to maintain that privacy is of key importance in its business strategies, mentioning the word 35 times in its IPO filing. Part of the reason Facebook can garner so much advertising revenue is due to its ability to target ads to users based on demographics and other information it has about its users. That data, according to Facebook, is not released to advertisers as it relates to individual users. Users would need to interact with the ad in order to engage with the advertiser.

Adding to its service, in September of 2011, Facebook announced Timeline and began rolling it out in December of that year. Prior to Timeline, older Facebook posts scrolled off the bottom of the page, so to speak, and were not easy to access. With Timeline, Facebook is making it easier for users to have a much broader profile and to track important life events and best moments. Facebook describes it as "a home for all the great stories you have already shared. They don't just vanish as you add new stuff." It is basically a digital resume. And therein resides a caution: There is no way to get rid of it once you move your profile to Timeline. However, individual posts can be tagged "Me Only," meaning they are not visible to anyone except the user, possibly keeping that resume more palatable.

Facebook Timeline does offer the opportunity for brand pages to radically change their Facebook presence to a much more graphically rich experience. As of this writing, few, if any, have made that leap, although some mock-ups (not approved by the brands) were created by Mammoth Advertising and McCann Digital in Israel that show what these new pages could look like.[63] This does put more pressure

---

[63]*How Facebook Timeline Might Radically Change the Look of Brand Pages*, by Todd Wasserman, Mashable Business, September 27, 2011

on marketers to come up with compelling content. This is especially important since Facebook now includes an option for users to unmark a top story, helping Facebook automatically edit feeds to make them more relevant, with irrelevant (according to the user) updates having less visibility. As a brand owner, you don't want your story to be the one everyone unchecks! It means marketers will need to work a little harder to stay relevant as Facebook moves more from "message streaming" to "lifestreaming."

Although Facebook facts and figures change daily, they are worth reviewing. Simply search "Facebook Facts and Statistics" on Google to get current data. Here is the scoop as of this writing:

- More than 845 million active users at the end of December 2011 (this grew from 150 million in January of 2009)
- More than 425 million active users currently accessing Facebook through their mobile devices
- 50% of active users log on to Facebook in any given day
- People spend over 700 billion minutes per month on Facebook and more than 30 billion pieces of content (web links, news stories, blog posts, notes, photo albums, etc.) are shared each month
- Average user is connected to 80 community pages, groups and events
- More than 2.5 million web sites have integrated with Facebook, including over 80 of comScore's U.S. Top 100 web sites and over half of comScore's Global Top 100 web sites
- More than 700,000 local businesses have active Pages on Facebook
- About 80% of Facebook users are outside of the United States
- 2.7 billion comments and likes are posted each day in Q42011

Note: Since the filing of its IPO, Facebook has significantly trimmed the official statistics it posts. The above list is a composite of statistics currently listed on the company's site and those that were listed prior to its IPO filing.

In addition to business pages on Facebook, many companies also often have evangelists who have their own Facebook and Twitter accounts, build their own online identities, gain their own followers, and can help promote online visibility of the company.

Caution: Be sure it is clear who owns these "evangelist" accounts and their followers. What happens when and if the individual evangelist leaves your employ? There have been recent lawsuits over just this topic, and by legally establishing ownership, you can avoid those types of problems in the future.

LinkedIn

LinkedIn is an interconnected network of professionals that, as of February 9, 2012, had more than 150 million members in over 200 countries and territories around the world, with 60% of the members being outside the U.S. There were more than four billion people searches on LinkedIn in 2011, up from two billion in 2010. As of December 31, 2011, mobile page views accounted for more than 15% of total member visits to LinkedIn.

The company claims that more than two new members join LinkedIn approximately every second and more than two million companies have LinkedIn company pages. It is worth noting that according to LinkedIn, executives from all 2011 Fortune 500 companies are LinkedIn members and its corporate hiring solutions are used by 75 of the Fortune 100 companies.

According to comScore, LinkedIn ranked as the 34th most visited website worldwide in the third quarter of 2011, up from 54th the prior year.

LinkedIn allows registered users to maintain a list of contact details of people they know and trust in business. This builds up a contact network, and allows users to see connections of their connections (called second-degree connections). This can be utilized to gain introductions through a mutual, trusted friend. Users can also recommend other users, and these recommendations can be leveraged for various purposes. Users can find, be introduced to and collaborate with qualified professionals they need to work with to accomplish their goals.

LinkedIn also allows users to research companies that they may be interested in working with or for. When typing the name of a given company in the search box, statistics about the company are provided, as well as employees of that company registered with LinkedIn and their relationship (if any) to the user's network. Company sites can contain specific information about their products and services as well.

According to comScore, unique visitors to the site averaged 87.6 million in the third quarter of 2011.

At first glance, LinkedIn may appear to be a site that is useful for a job search or a way to rub shoulders with fellow colleagues. But it has evolved into so much more. You can update your profile page with your RSS feed, be "introduced" to new connections, join groups and ask questions. The atmosphere is definitely more professional in nature than Facebook, and it's the perfect addition to your social media efforts. A good way to get started with LinkedIn is to join groups and participate - demonstrate your company's and your own attributes. Engage in the group; show yourself as a thought leader. You can also start your own group(s) to foster discussion about topics of interest to you and your customers/prospects.

Wait, There's More ...

In addition to these sites, you should definitely consider establishing a blog. You can also begin to dip your toe into location-based marketing. And don't forget video—not only should you consider placing brief video clips on your website—perhaps as a tutorial relevant to your business and your customers' needs, or as an explanation of a unique service you offer—but you can also easily produce and post videos on your own YouTube channel. Read on.

Scan the QR Code to watch a video on blogging.

foursquare

foursquare is one of an emerging class of location-based services. It is a mobile application that makes cities easier and more interesting to explore. It is a friend-finder, a city social guide and a game that challenges users to experience new things while rewarding them for doing so. foursquare lets users "check in" to a place when they're there, tell friends where they are and track the history of where they've been and who they've been there with.

As of December 2011, foursquare was reporting over 15 million users worldwide (about half in the U.S.), with more than 4 million check-ins per day. There are more than 600,000 businesses using the site's Merchant Platform, a free set of tools that helps businesses offer products, attract new customers and keep the best customers coming back. Registered users can connect with friends and update their location. Points are awarded for checking in at venues. Users can also earn badges by checking in at locations with certain tags, for check-in frequency or for other patterns, such as time of check-in. Users that check in the most times to a location, with a limit of one check-in per day, over a 60-day period are awarded the "mayorship" of the location until someone else succeeds them by checking in more times.

One example of how foursquare is being used in a business sense was CNN's partnership with the site to promote a week-long series on healthy eating. During the promotion, "If you friend CNN on foursquare and check in at one of 10,651 farmers markets across the globe, you'll get a 'Healthy Eater' badge." Dennis Crowley, the CEO of foursquare, said, "We've seen time and time again how foursquare can be used to drive people to action, and CNN's campaign is a perfect example of how brands can use the platform to promote good behavior, such as healthy eating."

In 2011, foursquare added two more important features, Explore (in March) and Radar (in October). With Explore, users can ask foursquare for information, such as, "where is the nearest coffee shop," based on their current location. With Radar, foursquare can buzz the user's phone, based on what foursquare knows the user likes to do, and tell them about things they ought to pay attention to in their current location. Radar gives local businesses another way to engage with customers on foursquare without having to wait for them to check in.

In addition, there are a number of apps that integrate with foursquare. For example, Don't Eat At was developed by NYU student Max Stoller following New York City's making public the health code violations of the City's restaurants. With Don't Eat At, when a foursquare user checks in at a restaurant, she can receive a message about the state of the restaurant's violations.

Thus foursquare is moving beyond the "check-in" phase to being a true location-based service that offers benefits to both businesses and to consumers.

As growth in mobile use continues with devices such as the Apple iPhone and iPad, Android phones and other GPS-enabled devices, marketers will increasingly look to location-based marketing for improved results. By experimenting with sites like foursquare and other location-based social media venues, like Yelp, you will gain insight into the possibilities these emerging services present.

YouTube

YouTube is a video-sharing web site owned by Google. Users can upload videos to share, and companies can establish "YouTube Channels." Founded in May of 2005, YouTube has partnership deals with content providers including major TV networks, music companies, etc. YouTube videos can "go viral," meaning people watch them, find them interesting, educational or amusing, and forward the link to friends. You may remember the series of "Will It Blend?" videos posted by blender manufacturer Blendtec in which founder Tom Dickson attempts to blend a number of unusual items in order to show the power of his blender. As of January 17, 2013, the Blendtec series of videos had collected a total of over 220 million views on YouTube.

We call this "humanizing" your brand. Today, people are less inclined to do business with a company simply because of their logo or because they recognize the brand. Before they open their wallet, they want to know who is behind the curtain. Video sites such as YouTube allow businesses to introduce their employees, passions, and interests to prospects and customers in a fun way.

48 hours of video are uploaded to YouTube every minute—that's eight years of content uploaded every day! More video is uploaded to YouTube in 60 days than the three major U.S. networks created in 60 years! Eight hundred million unique users visit YouTube each month. More than 50% of videos on YouTube have been rated by viewers or include comments from the community.

YouTube can be a powerful marketing platform if used correctly. A few hints:

- Don't make every video a marketing piece. Your YouTube channel should be a good mix of funny, behind-the-scenes, helpful…with a pinch of self-promotion. If you make every video like it's a commercial for your business, it's a sure fire way to NOT have your videos shared.

- Think outside the box, but not so far outside that your channel doesn't mesh with your brand.

- Keep it fresh and keep it short whenever possible. No one wants to watch something drag on and on. These days, few people have the luxury of time.

- Don't expect a lot of obvious, immediate return. Like much of your marketing efforts, this is just one more weapon in your arsenal. And in this same vein, don't base your opinion that a single video or your YouTube channel as a whole is a success or failure based on number of views. Yes, it's all a numbers game. But it also matters who sees it and what they do after they see it. Like other social media platforms, it's one more way to engage your audience.

Google+

Google+ is a social network that was launched in the 2nd-half of 2011 to much fanfare. According to comScore, Google+ attracted 67 million visitors to its site in November 2011. In December 2011, its U.S. visitors were up 55% over November of the same year, at 49 million, according to a Tweet from Experian Hitwise. It took Facebook four years to reach 60 million members, and Google+ has surpassed that in just a few months. Estimates are that the site will exceed 400 million members by the end of 2012, half the size of Facebook already.

While it contains similar features to Facebook and Twitter, simply having Google's backing makes it a social network worth paying attention to. (It seems that they have learned some valuable lessons from previous failures, including their Wave product!).For another data point, analytics firm Chitika estimates Google+ had as many as 62 million users by the end of 2011—from zero to 62 million in less than half a year is not bad by anyone's measure! Within three weeks of launch, Google+ had seen 20 million unique visitors. At that time, you could only access Google+ by invitation, which probably acted to increase the cachet of being part of something new and something Googley.

Although the site continues to grow exponentially, it is still in its infancy. Google+ is a site to watch in 2013 and beyond.

Blogs

Blog is a contraction of the term "web log." A blog is a web site that is generally maintained by an individual with regular entries of commentary, descriptions of events or other material such as graphics or videos. In addition to these personal blogs, there are also corporate blogs, and most news outlets these days also have blogs, often with entries written by their leading columnists or commentators.

Blogs are an excellent means of getting a discussion going. While it requires an authorized author to start a discussion track, anyone can post comments to a blog entry, and in the "blogosphere", or universe of blog readers and users, people are not typically shy about sharing their opinions on whatever topic is being discussed. Blogs can be moderated, meaning that an administrator reviews all comments before they go live. This allows you to prevent objectionable material from being posted to your blog. Be careful, however, in your censorship efforts, as we have advised before.

Blogging is one of the hallmarks of inbound marketing. Inbound marketing is a belief that creating good content – generally on a blog – will drive qualified leads to your website. These leads consume this content and "pay" for it with their contact information as currency.

Inbound marketing tactics are then fueled by outbound tactics, i.e., social networks. Creating new content is great, but if no one is reading it, what's the point? It is important for outbound channels to disseminate the materials your company creates. This brings in qualified leads, fills the sales funnel, generates revenue, and allows you to create more content. And the wheel keeps spinning.

BlogPulse reports that as of early January 2012, there were a total of 181 million identified blogs.

Technorati has issued an annual State of the Blogosphere study since 2004. In its 2011 report (the most recent as of this writing), the company classifies bloggers into four categories:

- Hobbyist (60% of respondents to the study). These bloggers blog for fun and do not report income from blogging. Their primary metric for success is personal satisfaction.
- Professional Part- and Full-Timers (18%). These are independent bloggers who either use blogging as a way to supplement their income or consider it their full-time job.
- Corporate (8%). These folks blog as part of their full-time job, or blog full-time for a company or organization they work for. 63% of corporate bloggers use their number of unique visitors to measure success.

- Entrepreneurs (13%). These are individuals blogging for a company or organization they own, primarily blogging about the industry they work in. They blog to share expertise, gain professional recognition and to attract new clients for their business.

Technorati reports that of the 14% of bloggers who earn a salary for blogging, the average annual amount is about $24 thousand. Corporate bloggers earn slightly more. Display ads, affiliate marketing links and search ads are the most common ways bloggers generate revenue from their blogs. The survey revealed that 53% of self-employed and 30% of professional part-timers did not earn revenue from their blogs; rather, most blog-related revenue is generated through giving speeches on blogging topics and advertising.

Universal McCann reports that 77% of Internet users read blogs.

Twitter Basics for Marketers

If you haven't already checked out Twitter and created a profile, what are you waiting for? Twitter is an excellent micro-blogging platform for spreading the word about company news, special events, discounts and more. Want to connect with prospects? Want to display your expertise? In 140 characters or less you can "tweet" tips, coupon codes, links to press releases…the sky is the limit. Here are some tips on how you can set your business up for success on Twitter.

Setting up your profile

Make sure you complete your profile. It needs to represent your company and further your brand, so upload your logo to use as your avatar.[64] Choose a Twitter name that is either your actual company

[64]An avatar is a computer user's representation of himself/herself or alter ego whether in the form of a three-dimensional model used in computer games,a two-dimensional icon (picture) or a one-dimensional username used on Internet forums and other communities. Source: Wikipedia, September 2010.

name, or an easy-to-understand shorter version of your company name. Your one-line bio allows for 160 characters only, so try to use keywords that make your profile searchable, rather than a vague tagline or slogan. You may want to create a custom background for your Twitter page that utilizes your logo in some way and have it clearly show the web address of your company web site. If you choose to have individuals act as evangelists for you on Twitter, they should use their own photos as their avatars.

Finding people to follow

After you set up your Twitter profile, you want to "follow" other Twitter users. This allows you to see their tweets from your Twitter home page. As you follow others, you will find that many follow you back. You want to build up your list of followers, because these are people who will be able to regularly see your tweets as you make them.

Finding people to follow isn't difficult. Some of your customers may actually invite you to follow them, by placing a Twitter badge on their website or adding their Twitter profile URL to their email signature. You can also click on the "Find People" link at the top of the Twitter page. From there, you have several options: find people on Twitter via their name, business name, brand, keyword or Twitter handle (user name); find people via other networks such as Google, Yahoo! or AOL; invite people via email; or look at suggested users.

After you begin following people and businesses you already know, you can:

- Check out the followers of those Twitter users you admire. If you are following someone or a company and you like their tweets and admire the way they handle themselves online, then it makes sense to see who they are following and do so as well.

- Use the "find people" search option and search with keywords that your target market would use in their Twitter handles and profiles.

Using Hashtags

Another way to grow your visibility on Twitter and to engage with like-minded people and organization is to use hashtags. A hashtag is a word or phrase preceded by the pound, or hash, sign (#). Including one or more hashtags in a Tweet designates a topic or area of interest that others might be following, such as #print, #marketing or #HigherEd. This extends your reach because users following those hashtags will pick up your Tweet and may follow you—and you can follow them back. Hashtags are also used in TweetChats or TweetJams—sessions about a specific topic carried out over a specific period of time. Participants can follow the conversation and join in by monitoring/ using the appropriate hashtag. Check out the hashtags your customers, competitors, followers and those you follow are using, and use them judiciously. You can also make up your own hashtags—though it is recommended that you search to see if they are already in use and in what context before you start using what you think is a new hashtag. You don't want to inadvertently get caught up in a porn network or anything like that!

Tweet responsibly and responsively

You'll need to be creative at times to get your message down to 140 characters or less. In fact, your goal should be to make your tweet shorter so that others can "re-tweet" your message without editing… getting it more exposure. It's okay to toot your own horn, but try to make sure your Twitter stream isn't a constant barrage of sales pitches. And make sure to keep an eye on your messages. You may receive private messages via the "Direct Message" system, or you may receive a public tweet when someone includes your Twitter handle in a tweet. You should respond in kind when appropriate – no one likes a tweeter who only tweets about their own stuff. It's customary to publicly or privately thank folks for mentioning you or retweeting one of your tweets. Keep in mind that Twitter is a conversational tool, not a one-way onslaught of your promotional tweets.

What to tweet about

There's plenty to tweet about. Here are some ideas:

- Links to your blog posts
- Links to your video or audio offerings
- Links to other online information (stats, blog posts, news articles/stories, videos, etc.) that you feel will berelevant, interesting or useful to your followers
- Company announcements – from employee of the month to hitting your latest sales goal
- What you are currently working on
- What you are currently reading
- Events you are attending or organizing
- Retweet other tweets to cultivate relationships and help disseminate useful information
- Answers to questions that relate to your business, products/services
- Ask questions and invite commentary

Facebook Basics for Marketers

Are you Facebooking your prospects and customers? With today's technology and the multiple ways you can interact with your prospects toget your message across, it's important to take advantage of the more popular social media sites where your prospects and customers hang out. Facebook has over 845 million users. Don't you think your current and future customers are among them? So if you haven't done so already, stop putting off the inevitable and set up a Facebook business page so you can connect with prospects and customers, promote your products/services, and make the most of the content you put out (articles, videos, audios, etc.) about your products and services. Be sure to look into Facebook Timeline to see how you might be able to enhance your company page using this new medium.

Keep in mind that there is a difference between personal and business accounts on Facebook. Business accounts are limited in the information they are able to access compared to standard accounts. You can't send or receive friend requests, for example. However, this shouldn't prevent you from creating a business page for your company. In fact, there are benefits to business pages, where you can designate multiple administrators to manage and post to the account. Also, the pages are public and therefore will attain rank in Facebook and search engine results. A business page can garner "Likes" and you can post events, pictures, videos, polls and other interactive ways to promote your business and build the buzz.

After you create your Facebook business page, you want people to "Like" your site. Here are some ways you can build that base:

- Make sure your page is searchable by the general public. This is typically the default setting, but you may want to double-check by looking at Settings on the Edit page. Make sure your page is "Published" (publicly visible).
- Announce your new Facebook page on your web site / blog with a link to your page and an invitation to "Like" your page.
- If you have a newsletter, be sure to include the news about your new Facebook page.
- Send out an email to all your existing contacts asking them to check out your Facebook page, "Like" it and leave a post.
- Leverage your other social media profiles and invite those connections and followers to check you out on Facebook. For example, if you're active on Twitter, you should tweet the link to your Facebook page and ask your followers to "Like" your page.
- Post a Facebook badge or widget on your website, in your newsletters, on your blog and in other communications to let people know about your Facebook page.
- Think about using Facebook ads. Yes, it costs some money, but the advertising will get your business name in front of a lot of eyeballs.

Of course, it will be easier to get more "Likes" as you build your page and add content that is informative and engaging. Add polls, events, links and videos. Invite commentary by posting questions. Pull in the RSS feed from your blog. Post about special discounts or coupons. As you build on your page, current followers will share the page with their colleagues and friends and your base will grow.

One thing you may want to avoid doing is having your twitter feed run on your Facebook page. Twitter users are used to a certain amount of fast paced tweets. Your viewers on Facebook may not appreciate an onslaught of mini posts automatically feeding into your Facebook page. Every so often, you can invite your Facebook audience to check you out on Twitter. And yes, there are some tweets that are more than appropriate to "repeat" as a post on your Facebook page. But as tempting as it may be to tie the two together, I suggest you don't.

Remember, Facebook is not just about information or entertainment. It's also about relationship building. Connect with your followers and respond to any posts by prospects and customers. It's important to create a dialog with your followers, rather than just have a running monologue of business information.

LinkedIn Basics for Marketers

LinkedIn has always been a business-oriented social networking site. As such, it's a natural place to set up shop and create a presence to connect with other businesses. It helps you to keep in touch with colleagues and customers, find experts, or show off your own expertise. LinkedIn allows you to interact and network with other professionals from around the globe. So where do you start?

Begin by building your business profile; make sure it is complete. You want to put your best foot forward and further your brand. So upload that logo, and in the Summary and Specialties section, remember to use plenty of keywords to make your business searchable. You can also add descriptions of products and services that will inform visitors about what you do. You will also want to make sure that key employees are LinkedIn members and that they show up on your page as employees of your company.

Once your profile is ready to go, it's time to make connections. You have several different options to grow your network. First, you can use webmail import to see who is in your email contact list that is already on LinkedIn. You can also upload your contacts from Outlook, Palm, ACT! and Mac Address. Then you can search for any companies you currently do business with or have had contact with in the past to see if they have a LinkedIn profile. Once you get connected, you can look at that person/company and their connections and gain introductions in order to widen your network. You can also send out invite emails to anyone you can't find on LinkedIn, but would like to connect with. LinkedIn will also suggest other users you may wish to link to. Be sure to peruse that list periodically to see who else may have joined. Remember, every time you link to someone it expands your network not by one, but by however many first degree connections that person has!

Once you have your profile set up and some connections are made, look through your connections to see if there are any customers you could ask to give you a recommendation. This is basically a testimonial that will show up on your LinkedIn page and will help build your credibility. You should also examine who you are connected to that could benefit from a recommendation from you. Don't hesitate to start the ball rolling and spread the testimonial love by leaving positive feedback on the recommendation form for your connections.

Become a joiner by checking out LinkedIn Groups. You can search using keywords to find some groups where you can exchange ideas with colleagues or establish your expertise with your target market. Pick a few and prepare to be active, posting news articles or inserting yourself into the middle of an online discussion. Once you have some group experience under your belt, consider establishing your own group(s) in LinkedIn. If you do so, though, be sure that you keep content current. Don't just set it up and expect it to grow. As with all social media, you have to be proactive.

You can also build credibility and display your business know-how by answering questions. Browse the "Answers" section where you can post a thought-provoking question or find a question that you know the answer to. You can check out the various categories, or use the advanced search feature to drill down for more specific categories of questions.

You'll also want to visit the LinkedIn Applications page where you can look at the optional add-ons that can spice up your LinkedIn experience. You can add a reading list to show viewers books you suggest. Or you can embed a presentation. You can even sync your WordPress blog posts to your profile. Adding an application or three can definitely make your business stand out and draw more attention, so take some time to pick out a few that will really complement your LinkedIn profile.

To get the most out of your LinkedIn experience, make sure you log in, update your status and interact with your connections at least two to three times a week. You want to make sure your presence is obvious. If you never log in and engage others, answer or post questions or update your profile status, then you'll be missing out on the benefits of social media for your business.

URL-Shortening

One facet of many social media sites that marketers are forced to account for is the character-limit on the corresponding site. For example, Twitter only allows you to enter 140 characters.

To account for this, marketers are required to ensure that their messages only contain important words and phrases. But one more way to handle these limitations is to shorten URLs that you may include in your posts.

interlinkONE has built a tool—ilink.me—to help people do this. You can use it for free at http://www.ilink.me

URL-shortener tools like ilnk.me, bit.ly, tinyURL and others are easy to use. They can dramatically reduce the amount of characters in the URL that you are looking to share with others. But along with shortening the URL, these tools can also provide another great benefit: they enable you to track how many people are clicking on your links!

For example, let's say that you want to share a white paper with your social media fans, friends, and followers. The PDF of the white paper may exist on a web server, with a URL such as http://www.MyCompany.com/Resources/WhitePapers/SavingMoneyToday.pdf

If you place that in a URL-shortening tool, the resulting URL may be something like http://ilnk.me/75612

If you were to then post an entry on Twitter, such as "Check out our new white paper for tips on saving money at http://ilnk.me/75612," your URL-shortening tool would allow you to see how many people clicked the link from Twitter.

You could then create another short URL for that same white paper, and post that one on Facebook. You would receive a whole new set of reports for that URL, and that target audience. With tools like ilink.me, you can let the shortener automatically spit out a shortened URL, or you can create a name. This is especially helpful when you want to keep track of a few different links and prefer to name the shortened version yourself. You can also have it set up to email you when the link is clicked on. Tactics like this can help you compare how effectively certain social media sites are working for you.

Building a Social Media Plan

Like anything in business or marketing, you have better success if you have a plan in place. Strategy before tactics is worth repeating here. Your marketing plan needs an online marketing elementto include social media. Tweets, Facebook posts and the likeshould not be left up to Benjaminthe receptionist who is good at Facebook

This checklist will guide you in making your social media experience successful and can be the basis for building your social media plan. It makes mention of a few sites we haven't discussed, so be sure to check them out.

A company representative should be active on two to four different social media sites on a daily/weekly basis in order to connect with others and build relationships.

- LinkedIn
- Twitter
- Facebook
- Google+
- YouTube
- Flickr

Items to post:

- Behind the scenes pictures
- Client success stories & Testimonials
- Press releases
- Articles
- Podcasts
- Answers to frequently asked questions
- Questions (to invite answers/comments from others)
- Company announcements & upcoming events & specials
- How-to videos & Tips to help your prospects and clients
- Contests & giveaways

Want to look at a huge list of social media sites by category? You might be able to find a couple of sites where your prospects hang out…a good place for you to network! Check out: http://ilnk.me/SocialWeb or scan to receive the list:

Figure 7. Having a Plan Helps You Get Noticed

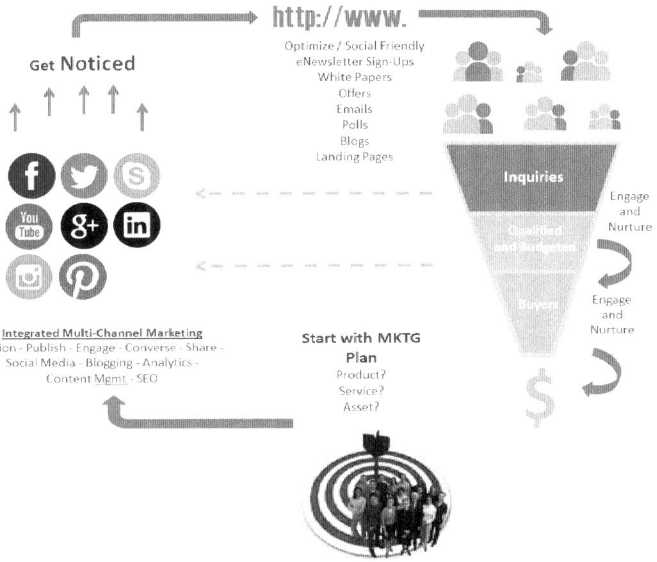

Figure 7 demonstrates why social media activities will only succeed with a plan --- there are so many channels, but when used properly, they can lead to new sales.

> For more information on inbound marketing, download our White Paper at http://ilink.me/InbdMktg.

Do You Know the Score?

Now that you are into the world of social media, how do you rate your performance? Part of this rating will depend on the goals and objectives you set for your social media initiatives. These can include revenue goals, numbers of followers, unique visitors, number and frequency of comments, those types of things. And these are important metrics to follow, especially as you are likely to need to seek additional funding for these efforts from time to time. The boardroom and C-suite want results for their dollars!

You can also turn to outside sources to rate your performance. These would be services such as Tweet Grader (tweet.grader.com) which allows you to measure the power of your Twitter profile compared to millions of other users that have been graded. You simply enter your Twitter user name and click "Grade." You can also enter other Twitter user names to see how they rank, a good way to keep tabs on your competition.

Another tool is Klout, which allows you to connect your Twitter, Facebook, LinkedIn and Google+ accounts to get a view of your overall "klout" in the social media sphere. Using available data, it measures the size of a person's network, the content created and how other people interact with that content. When you sign up for Klout, you authorize these connections with your social media accounts. Klout ranks you on a scale of 1 to 100; 20 is about average, and anything above 30 is reputable. Above 50 would be considered elite.

Now is the Time!

There is a great deal to digest in this chapter, especially if you have not yet started using social media, personally or professionally, on a regular basis. Don't be intimidated. It is easier than it may sound. But also, don't put off this important step. Once you get your feet wet, I have no doubt that you and your staff will have many, many great ideas about how to use social media for your own business purposes.

So far in this book, we have been talking about the past and present. Now let's turn our attention to the future of our businesses.

Chapter Seven: Building an Untethered Marketing Strategy

If you're not talking to your customers, you're just guessing from a conference room.

This chapter will focus specifically on how to build an untethered marketing strategy. This strategy should be incorporated into your overall marketing plan, which is an element of your business plan. If you don't already have a business/marketing plan in place, please create them in conjunction with the untethered plan! Both are critical to running a successful business. It always surprises me how many businesses do not have written business and marketing plans in place to guide their short- and long-term operations, investments and strategies.

Setting the Stage

There are myriad books and web sites available to help you build your base business/marketing plan if you don't already have one. Alternatively, you can purchase a copy of my first book, *Business Transformation: A New Path to Profit for the Printing Industry*. While I wrote that one specifically for the printing industry, the business and marketing planning sections are, with only minor modifications, applicable to any type of business, and will give you a turnkey approach for developing those plans. You can purchase the book by visiting http://ilink.me/MarcomU.

If you already have both business and marketing plans in place, now is a good time to review them to ensure they are up to date, and during that process, to incorporate the untethered concepts we are discussing here.

Building an untethered marketing plan is the first step in identifying how the mobile audience will connect with you and your marketing communications. I'm not suggesting that you throw the baby out with bathwater, especially if you have a functional marketing plan in place. I am suggesting, though, that you take a good look at your existing plans and strategies and how they mesh with a new untethered approach. Likely, many if not all of your current strategies and tactics will still be valid, and will be even more effective once you weave in the untethered aspects we are recommending here. But in some cases, you will want to revamp the process completely, especially if you have not recently updated your plans, and this is a good time to do so.

This is especially true if you have not implemented an integrated multichannel marketing plan; that is, if you have primarily been relying on a certain set of media as independent, standalone activities. For many smaller businesses, this might include Yellow Pages advertising, newspaper or trade magazine advertising, perhaps an email newsletter and some direct mail or radio advertising. These are all still good strategies (well, not sure about Yellow Pages these days!), but to the extent they are integrated into one campaign that leverages the strengths of each of the various media and creates multiple touches with common messaging, your results will be exponentially stronger.

The other aspect of an untethered marketing plan will be the need to monitor campaign and communications results and activities in real time, and to be able to respond in real time or near real time. People responding to a magazine, radio or newspaper ad may not have the same expectations about response time as someone who is responding to an SMS message on their phone, or who has gone to a personalized web microsite in response to an offer, or even has sent a message—broadcast or direct—through Twitter. Expectations here are that someone will be monitoring these channels and will respond quickly.

A great example here—one everyone is probably sick of hearing about because it has been written about so much, but I am going to cite it anyway—is Zappos. If you follow them on Twitter, you will see that when one customer service rep checks out for the day, he or she introduces the next one up, and that person then sends a personal message letting followers know who's on board next to help. Here is an example of a "check-in/check-out", received within a few seconds of each other:

"@Zappos_Service: Okay, everyone. Erik is out for the night. Please welcome the always-awesome Sarah!"

"@Zappos_Service: Hey all! It's Sarah. Happy Friday!"

This offers customers/prospects/followers a personal connection to the company and instant response to queries. This approach might be a bit over the top for many companies, but it is a good example of what can be done with social media if your customer relationships justify that type of "in your face" immediacy.

Another aspect of using a variety of touch points, beyond building relationships and making the customer or prospect feel special, is the ability to track results. By integrating all of your channels, you can set up a holistic look at all of them, and enable processes for immediate response.

A Case in Point

Let's use a car dealership as an example. The campaign might start with a postcard mailing to a list of prospects announcing the availability of the new BMW 3-Series. Each postcard has a QR Code and/or a link to a personalized URL. First of all, by putting the correct USPS barcodes on the mailing—Intelligent Mail Barcode or IMB—you can track the mailing all the way to the recipient's mailbox, so you know when the mail drops and when it is received at the other end, as well as other data along the way. This might be followed by an email that is scheduled to be delivered two to three days after the mail hits the household. When the recipient responds by snapping the QR code or typing or clicking the personalized URL, that action is also recorded.

Once the person reaches the microsite, the visitor is asked to complete a very brief survey (collecting information to enable the creation of more relevant communications), and then several options are displayed, perhaps even based on the survey responses (you can do that with the right solution in place! Talk about real time!).

In our example, the prospect chooses to watch a 3-Series video. That action is logged, but more importantly, the relevant sales representative receives an email or text message indicating that the action has happened. That, in turn, can generate a call to the visitor that might get them into the sales show room for a test drive. Because the sales rep is receiving messages on his smartphone, he can respond from anywhere, even from the beach on his day off, if he so chooses (though we want to keep in mind employee health and well-being as we discussed in Chapter Five!)

Let's assume our recipient is so excited about all of this special treatment that she decides to visit the showroom for a test drive, but doesn't make a buying decision that day. Our trusty sales rep has taken a photo of her in or beside the car, and follows up with a Postagram postcard created with that photo, thanking her for visiting and lining up the next step in the sales cycle.

Clearly, you don't want to appear to be stalking your prospects, but you do want to show that you care about them and their business, and you do want to make the communications as customized as possible. Finally, you do want to track everything that happens and record those actions in a database. This is just one example of how that could be done.

The Importance of Response Mechanisms

The key to an effective untethered marketing approach is the ability of customers and prospects to be able to interact with your marketing campaign. In the BMW example we just used, even the print element is interactive because of the QR Code and/or personalized URL. We have made it easy for recipients to take an action—snapping the QR Code—and take the next step toward engaging in a dialog. The landing page to which they are directed must be optimized for web and mobile since you won't know which platform they are going to use and you shouldn't really care. These should be designed with a mobile-first strategy, not a one-size-fits-all approach. In the process of designing the campaign, think about all of the different ways people might be communicating and how to make it as easy as possible for them to interact with your campaign.

Remember the Philly Peapod example in Chapter Three? That's an example of a convenient engagement point. In this case, they will be using a mobile device just by the very nature of the interaction. The user may be an existing Peapod customer or a new customer. The mobile interface should allow them to log in or to set up an account, as a starter. Once they have activated the mobile app, there should be an option for the app to remember them—the next time they use it, it automatically logs them in, making the transaction even faster and more convenient. Perhaps the next step for Peapod would be to extend the campaign using free-standing inserts (FSIs) in the Sunday paper. Talk about your couch potato shopping from home!

Regardless of the approach—or combination of approaches—you choose to take, response mechanisms should be many, intuitive, and built for both web and mobile (and even maybe phone and mail!).

Another way to engage potential customers is through the use of games and sweepstakes. Think about how to design a fun mobile app that incorporates a game that also has in-app sales—either for a paid version of the app, or for some sort of product or service related to the app, such as a magazine subscription. The key is to find a way to engage the prospect and get that dialog going. And the app should also interact with any ongoing campaigns you have. Give users an opportunity to automatically have the app updated so they are sure they are getting the latest and greatest offers. Use geo-location and/or geo fencing to make the interaction geographically relevant as well. All of the things we have been discussing thus far are relevant here.

If you are conducting an event, perhaps you want

an application specifically for that occasion. They can register for the event, they can access agendas, programs and speaker bios, sign up for newsletters, find out where particular sessions are, even have the opportunity to interact with speakers on some level, and to tweet or post to Facebook about their experience.

Engage, engage, engage. That's really the mantra for marketing today, and especially for an untethered marketing strategy. Make it easy for your audience to respond in an untethered manner, or from a laptop or desktop if that is what they choose. They are in the driver's seat, and that must be recognized.

This bears repeating: Mobile is an extension of your overall marketing plan, but you still should have an overarching business plan of which your marketing plan is a part. As we proceed in this chapter, we will be focusing on your untethered marketing plan, the mobile aspect only. But take the opportunity to review your existing marketing plan, make necessary changes, and smoothly incorporate the untethered aspect.

Moving from Mobile Friendly to Mobile First

As we have been discussing, in today's untethered world, it is simply not acceptable to consumers to have to access a standard web site from a mobile device. They expect web sites these days to be mobile friendly. But for many marketers, even mobile friendly is not enough. Many are rapidly moving to mobile first. Let's take a few moments to address this topic before we move to the untethered marketing plan.

What do I mean by mobile first? First, let's refresh our thoughts on mobile friendly. For many companies, this meant "dumbing down" their regular web site, removing and resizing content to make it fit the screen. But that approach does not offer the opportunity to focus on what mobile users really want from a site. Nor does it do a good job of facilitating engagement. Sure, the information is there for those who are looking. The key difference between PC users and mobile users is that mobile users are focused. PC users are generally multitasking between work, play and casual research. Mobile users are on the go and want fast answers. They are also usually transaction-oriented. They may be looking to buy a specific item, compare prices, find a location nearby that carries something they are interested in—and they are not willing to dig through layers of web content to get that information. If your site doesn't offer what they are looking for, a competitor's surely does!

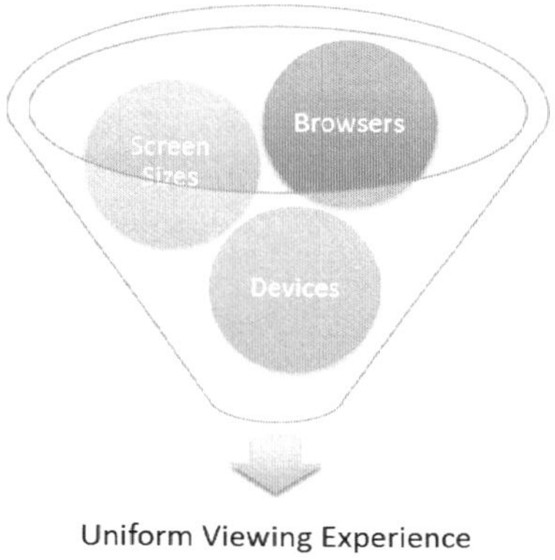

And you also can't assume that something designed for a mobile phone will also be appropriate for a tablet. Tablet users fall somewhere in between PC and smartphone users. They are focused in the sense that they are focused on the tablet experience, and the depth of rich content they can get via that medium. They are likely not multitasking as much as a PC user would be. But they are willing to take more time and gain a broader experience than the average smartphone user. So perhaps they would like to see a video of your product, or watch a video interview of one of your executives or customers. If you are a restaurant owner, they might want to peruse your menu or wine list and get details about other offerings. A smartphone user is more likely to want to make a reservation, look up directions, or take a quick—one could say superficial—look at the menu.

Responsive Web Design

This is where a relatively new technique comes in: Responsive web design. This is the concept of developing a web site in a style that allows the layout to change based on the user's screen resolution. It is a completely different approach from traditional web design. For example, if the user accesses a web site from a PC, they might see a four-column design, while the same site accessed from a smartphone might be automatically simplified into two columns or even a single column. User choices can vary from PC to tablet to mobile.

This is a mobile-first approach. From the outset, the design assumes the site will be accessed by some type of mobile device, but also leaves the door open for desktop/laptop access, serving the specific needs of all of these users.

Keep in mind that smartphone users are averse to complex navigation paths. In addition, as of the date of this writing, Flash is still not supported on Apple devices (in fact, Adobe is even backing away from Flash), so web designers should stay away from Flash, giving preference to HTML5. Pages should also load quickly, regardless of the device. Content consumers are an impatient lot—some experts suggest that even a one second delay in a site loading can result in a 7% reduction in conversion.

Mobile content should also be prioritized. Think about what your customers are most likely to do from a smartphone or a tablet, and organize content accordingly. Continuing with the restaurant example, perhaps the first choice the user sees is "make a reservation," the second choice might be "view our menu." Directions to the establishment and any daily specials or offers should also be readily accessible.

Also keep in mind that mobile users, whether tablet or smartphone, are more in tune with touch-and-swipe, while desktop/laptop users are usually point-and-click oriented. Your designs must take these differences into consideration.

The bottom line: mobile first means providing a consistent experience and brand image across all platforms, and understanding that mobile browsing is rapidly overtaking desktop browsing as the way in which consumers choose to interact with your brand, your product and your company.

Now, on to the untethered marketing plan!

The Untethered Marketing Plan

As a subset of your full marketing plan, certain common plan elements will be assumed. For example, the overview of your company and your target markets, overall goals and objectives and umbrella marketing strategy will be included in the parent marketing plan. Below are recommended sections for the untethered aspect of your marketing plan, placed in the form of questions (sometimes questions get you thinking a bit more!):

- Who is / are your target audience(s)? (if different from your primary marketing plan)
- What are the goals and objectives of your untethered communications strategy? (differences to your overall plan should be noted)
- Untethered marketing strategy: Why do you have one and what do you hope to achieve as a result?
- Startup and execution: how will you get your untethered marketing activities off the ground?
- Marketing Deliverables and Measures of Success: What will specifically be encompassed within this untethered marketing plan in terms of tactics designed to meet your overall marketing goals and objectives; how will you measure your success?
- Team member responsibilities: Who will be responsible for what inside this plan?Are they are internal or external resources?
- Sources of Content: By its very nature, an untethered marketing strategy moves fast. It is important to document specific content, or sources of content that you will use in execution of this plan. What information can you use to build your content resource library? What will you add to that library as time marches on? How will you offer it so it can be accessed for instant or scheduled delivery?
- Keywords: What are the keywords that are relevant to your business? Consider everything that makes sense, including misspellings, phrases in alternative order, etc. For example, if your business works with higher ed institutions to recruit students, you would include such keywords as recruit students, recruitment of students, student recruitment. Ask yourself what

would a user type into Google to find products or services like yours?

- Branding strategy: Since you will be working across a variety of media, how will you ensure brand integrity, both from a look-and-feel perspective as well as from a tone and message perspective?
- Public relations strategy: Public relations is the new "advertising." How will you incorporate not only traditional public relations activities which should be covered in your master marketing plan, but also includes web, email, social media and event activities?
- Mobile strategy: How will you access and address the various mobile devices now in the marketplace and coming soon? What apps will you develop and how you will market them? Will you focus on in-app sales, sales of apps, mobile payment strategies, customer acquisition, customer retention, etc.? (You're going to want to document revenue or other business results you expect to obtain specifically from mobile)
- Marketing Calendar: Do you know of all the different days, weeks and months celebrated around the world that can be used for promotional purposes? This should be a daily, detailed calendar that begins with documenting an entry for everyday of the year—holidays, special recognition days, product launches, events—anything that you could possibly communicate about or discuss with your audiences to drive engagement. A sample calendar can be found starting on page 126.

Sales Pitch Warning: My company, Grow Socially, is in the business of putting together untethered marketing plans. So if you do choose to outsource all or part of this work, think about contacting us. We would be happy to discuss how we can help!

For each section of the untethered marketing plan, we will pose questions that you should be asking yourself as you flesh out that section and make suggestions to get you started. Because every business is different, and because this plan should be very detailed, it is not possible or productive to provide a finished, detailed plan. However, where it makes sense, we will use real-world examples that will give more depth to the discussion.

Target Audiences

Who is your target market? Your target market(s) is likely to be similar to the target market(s) for your master marketing plan. You can target your market by vertical industries (manufacturing, financial services, higher education, real estate, government, etc.) or by horizontal applications—that is, solutions that apply across a range of different industries. You can further refine your target market by company size, and geographic location. Or if you are targeting consumers, look to age, gender, income range, education level, or even type of mobile device(s) owned. These would be the normal type of specifications for target audiences. What could be different here is targeting audiences by the type of device(s) they own or are most likely to use.

Other questions to ask about your audience:

- Where is your audience cyclically? Are there specific cycles when your audience is more likely to buy? Perhaps a specific holiday, on or around the tax season, or at the beginning or end of fiscal budget cycles? These cycles should be identified, along with the strongest months by audience. Why is this important? Particularly with social media, you will be able to get to those audiences at what Google calls The Zero Moment of Truth (ZMOT).[65] This is the online decision-making moment for which you want to be present. Understanding cyclically when your audience is most likely to be in a buying mood will give you a leg up in driving results for your business.
- Do you have a good feel for how your audience uses social media? You can gain this information in a variety of ways: Talking to existing customers, monitoring the social media activity of customers and prospects, and looking at how recent deals involving social media were instigated and closed.

[65]http://www.zeromomentoftruth.com/?locale=en_us

Goals and Objectives

Here you should list specific goals and objectives for your untethered marketing plan. These may reflect and augment goals and objectives contained in the master marketing plan, or they may be specific goals and objectives that are related to the untethered aspect of your marketing plan. Here are some example goals and objectives to get you started. You will need to refine them to specifically address your business requirements:

- Create sales through company website.
- Create and increase website traffic.
- Create search engine optimization results.
- Create brand awareness.
- Promote brand and message to target audience through multiple social media platforms.
- Direct people of interest and potential buyers to company's website.
- Create and encourage customer interaction.
- Create and manage online channels to promote the company and its products/services.
- Create the opportunity for the team members to connect with prospects.
- Create the opportunity for the team to build a reputation of being a quality informational resource and expert for their industry.

Untethered Marketing Strategy

As you think through this section of the plan, it is important to start with an established baseline. Where are you now with your social media presence? Document where you have a presence, how many Likes/Followers/Following you have, and any other relevant statistics. Here are some examples of what to look at:

- How many tweets have you sent out?
- How many different Twitter accounts are there representing your company?

- What blogs do you have and how frequently have you been posting?
- What level of comments are you seeing on your blog(s) and Facebook page(s)?
- Can people subscribe to your blog(s)? Are you set up to automatically "FaceTweetLink" a message when you post a new blog entry?
- Do you have a YouTube channel? If so, how many cumulative views do you have? Are there videos gaining more visibility than others? Can you figure out why and replicate that?
- Also document your baseline website statistics in this portion of your plan to act as a baseline—number of unique visitors, page views, average time spent per page, that sort of thing—assuming, of course, that you have a website! Use data from the previous month.

As you review your current presence, think about ways you can humanize your brand. Remember the Zappos example? Each customer service representative introduces himself/herself on Twitter and customers can feel like they are having a conversation with a real individual—because they are. You can also share photos, stories and videos about your staff and customers. Video case studies and testimonials are especially impactful, and much easier to produce today than ever before. While they should be of good quality, they do not need to have the high production value of, say, a television commercial.

You can also use your social media channels to share knowledge and company news. This should be an appropriate blend of thought leadership content and promotional content—with more emphasis on thought leadership and less on promotion. Too much promotional content will turn people off. Brainstorm with your team as to where to secure this content. It can be internally developed, it can be links to trade and other articles relevant to your audience, re-tweets or comments on postings by others, and it can even be something simply fun—but business appropriate.

Measuring Your Success

For each social media channel, you should set goals that challenge you and your team to exceed your current baseline. If you are starting from zero, don't set those goals too low! I have listed some of the metrics you can measure, by channel. Look at them monthly, weekly, daily—whichever makes the most sense for your business—and chart them to measure your progress. Include a goal line on each chart to make it easy to see when you have reached your established goal for that metric.

- Facebook
    - Number of Likes
    - Number of Interactions
    - Top Day for Interactions
    - Positive/Neutral/Negative Sentiment
    - Top Fan Pages (Likes)
    - Top Fan Pages (Posts/Comments)
    - Percentage of Referrals to Website
- Twitter
    - Number of Followers
    - Number of Retweets
    - Number of mentions
    - Number of Followers Who Interact
    - Top Day

Scan the QR Code to download this list so you can have it handy any time!

- Positive/Neutral/Negative Sentiment
- Top Influencers (By Volume)
- Top Influencers (By Impact)
- Percentage of Referrals to Website

- Blog
  - Number of posts per week/month
  - Average number of comments per post
  - Number of blog subscribers
  - Number of mentions on Twitter/Facebook
- LinkedIn
  - Number of Followers
  - Percentage of Referrals to Website
  - Number of Recommendations
- YouTube
  - Number of Subscribers
  - Number of Channel Views
  - Number of Video Views
  - Number of Comments
  - Percentage of Referrals to Website
  - Number of Subscribers
- Content
  - Most Popular Links of Each Month
  - Highlighted Social Interactions
- Website
  - Number of Visits
  - Number of Unique Visitors

- o Number of Page Views
- o Bounce Rate
- o Average Time on Site
- o Percentage of New Visits
- o Most Viewed Pages
- o Percentage of Direct Traffic
- o Percentage of Referring Sites (links in to your site will help your search engine ranking)
- o Percentage of Search Engines
- o Top Traffic Sources/Referral sites
    - Number of Visits from each source
    - Percentage of Visits from each source
    - Visits by Geography
- o Top Keywords Used to Find Your Site
    - Number of Visits from each keyword
    - Percentage of Visits from each keyword
- o Number of conversions
    - Forms completed and submitted (this could be Contact Us, Request Information, Register for Event, Download eBook or Whitepaper or any other call to action (CTA)
    - Videos viewed
    - Downloads (including white papers, brochures, etc.)
    - Sales
    - Requests for information

Strategies by Channel

You should also think about specific strategies or goals for each channel. What is it that you want to accomplish with that channel?

Once you have determined the strategies, you can then proceed to construct specific tactics designed to deliver against those strategies. Here are some examples to get you started.

- Facebook Strategies:
  - Increase "Likes" and drive traffic back to the website
  - Increase public awareness about the company
  - Build relationships with audience
  - Share information with audience
  - Engage in a dialog with audience
  - Use Facebook as a customer service channel for audience
  - Consider using Facebook ads
- Twitter Strategies:
  - Make it easy for your audience to voice concerns, pose questions or provide other feedback using Twitter; Initial contact might be public (someone should be consistently monitoring the Twitter feed and mentions), and conversations can be moved to private Direct Messaging or other communications means as appropriate
  - Share information with audience
  - Retweet and interact with audience
  - Promote the company and its products/services (be conservative here)
  - Find and engage people who may be interested in purchasing products/services
  - Find and engage with thought leaders
  - Find and incorporate keywords and hashtags into each Twitter post to help drive search and expand the reach of your tweets. Which hashtags are in most common use in your audience? Examine tweets from your followers and those you follow; expand your search by looking at tweets from your followers' followers. (Using hashtags

judiciously can be huge in expanding your reach and gaining search visibility)

- LinkedIn Strategies:
  - o Build a complete profile for your Company Page, including your logo as "avatar"
  - o Add products/services to the page
  - o Make sure all relevant company employees are LinkedIn members and show up on your page
  - o Seek recommendations from customers and others (industry experts, etc.) for posting on your Company Page
  - o Consider LinkedIn Ads as a possibility for the future
- Blog Strategies
  - o Build a plan for blog content but be flexible in order to address timely topics/issues
  - o Make sure blog titles, abstracts and content contain keywords relevant to your business
  - o Use at least one image in each blog post
  - o Associate metadata with your blog posts (including keywords) for more searchability
  - o Encourage visitors to subscribe to your blog and to comment on posts
  - o Seek ways to gain external links to your blog (This will raise its credibility with your audience and its visibility with search engines)
  - o FaceTweetLink blog posts for greater exposure using keywords and hashtags; this process can be automated
  - o Seek "guest bloggers" to contribute to your blog (These can be customers, employees, industry experts, etc.)
- YouTube Strategies:
  - o Create videos of:
    - Installing and using key products

    - Customer testimonials
    - Video contests
    - Campaigns
    - Product demos
    - Services overview and benefits
    - Share others' videos to entertain
  - Serve as a hosting platform for videos on the website
  - Have favorite videos
  - Subscribe to other channels
  - Encourage subscribers to your channel

Building a Mobile Strategy

We have talked a great deal about mobile-first in this book, and it is important in your untethered marketing plan to attack that head-on by having an explicit mobile strategy that establishes your company as a thought leader in this arena. You can utilize technologies such as QR Codes and other promotional strategies and campaigns to drive traffic to your mobile site, and make that site useful to the visitor, whether it is through informative videos, quick ways to engage with your business (making reservations, speaking with a customer service agent, etc. etc.) Here are some example elements of a mobile strategy to get you started:

Goals

- To reach the mobile audience
- To stand out as a thought leader for innovative tools and ideas
- To create more informative and interactive collateral

Mobile Landing Pages

- Promotional discount codes
- Surveys
- Enter-to-Win forms
- Blogs
- 'Contact Us' or 'Request More Information' forms
- Lead generation efforts
- Polls
- Product interest &download info

Locations for QR Codes

- Posters
- Direct mailers
- Business cards
- Envelopes
- Social media posts
- Tags and labels
- Coupons

Keep Messaging Fresh

To better achieve your goals and objectives, and to keep your audiences engaged, you must keep your messaging fresh. An annual messaging review, which might have been appropriate in the "old days," is simply not appropriate anymore, especially in an untethered marketing environment. Things move quickly. The market can change dramatically in a heartbeat. You must be seen as been savvy, in tune with the market, current with the news (both industry and otherwise), and aware of developments in the mobile and social media spheres. You must also been seen to capitalize on this awareness and savvy … in terms of your messaging, your online and mobile activity and the tweaking, relaunching, and development of your products and services. Never has the old saying been more applicable: Time is of the essence.

As you think about sources of content and information, especially as it relates to trends and issues relevant to your company and your audience(s), use tools such as Google Alerts, Google Reader, or Yahoo! Alerts to bring the news to you. By refining your Alerts and your Reader selections, you can keep the numbers reasonable. You don't want to be wading through thousands of listings on Google Reader every day! Start big and weed out sources that either have too much content, irrelevant content, or even inadequate relevant content. This can be done relatively quickly.

You can also find new sources of content by monitoring your Twitter feeds. Where are others getting their content? What types of links or stories are they tweeting/retweeting that could be of interest to your followers?

Here are a few additional ideas to get you started:

- Entertainment
  - YouTube videos
  - Photos
  - Blog posts
  - Outreach for interaction with pop culture figures

- o Utility
  - Customer Service Channel
  - Customer Outreach
- o Information
  - Blog posts that deliver information
  - How-To videos that relate to your products/services
  - How-To videos of how to order online
  - How-To videos of how to operate your products
  - Educational whitepapers or eBooks for downloading (seek out guest authors who have market recognition where possible)
- o Recognition
  - People who are using your product/services and how they are using them, especially if they are using them in innovative ways
    - Cool Stuff section
    - Photos
    - Videos
- o Loyalty Rewards
  - Contests

Calendar of Monthly Themes

By developing a calendar of monthly themes, you can more easily segment your content, prepare it or collect it, and schedule marketing activities around these themes. Again, every business is different, so you will need to think through topics and designated days/months/weeks that will resonate with your audiences. The examples below come from the healthcare industry and are U.S.-centric. Once you have outlined monthly themes, these can be utilized in subsequent years (although you should review for possible updates). From a tactical perspective, these themes will allow you to outline a content topic/theme/item for each day of the year and to assign resources to preparing your untethered (and tethered!) marketing messages/ activities/tactics.

- January
  - New Year
  - Martin Luther King, Jr. Day
  - Blood Donor Month
  - Eye Care Month
- February
  - Heart Month
  - Valentine's Day
  - Leap Year
  - Groundhog Day
  - Mardi Gras
  - President's Day
  - Wear Red Day
  - Children's Dental Health Month
  - Patient Recognition Week
- March
  - St. Patrick's Day
  - March Madness
  - Daylight Savings Time
  - Dr. Seuss's Birthday
  - Easter
  - Save your Vision Week
  - International Women's Day
  - First Day of Spring
  - Brain Awareness Week

  - Spring Cleaning Week
  - American Diabetes Alert Day
  - Baseball Spring Training
  - Nutrition Month
  - Ethics Awareness Month
  - Doctors Day
- April
  - Taxes Due
  - April Fool's Day
  - Opening Baseball Day
  - Osteoporosis Day Prevention
  - Oral Health Month
  - Alcohol Awareness Month
  - Stress Awareness Month
  - Occupational Therapy Month
  - Cancer Control Month
  - Humor Month
  - Public Health Week
  - Earth Day
  - Administrative Professionals Day
- May
  - Arthritis Awareness Month
  - Cancer Research Month
  - Nurses Week
  - Cinco de Mayo
  - Physical Fitness and Sports month
  - Lou Gehrig Disease Awareness Month

- Foster Care Month
- Bike Safety Month
- Teacher Appreciation Week
- Memorial Day
- Graduation
- Mother's Day

- June
    - Paul Bunyon Day
    - Graduation
    - Father's Day
    - Yoga Awareness Month
    - Safety Month
    - Men's Health Week
    - Flag Day
    - Candy Month
    - Sun Safety Month
    - World Environment Day
    - Nursing Assistants Week
    - Summer
- July
    - Juvenile Arthritis Awareness Month
    - 4th of July
    - Parents Day
    - Social Wellness Month
    - Family Reunion Month
    - Cell Phone Courtesy Month
    - Recreation & Parks Month

- Independence Day
- Therapeutic Recreation Week
- Ice Cream Day
- Hug Your Kids Day

• August

- Back to School
- Immunization Awareness Month
- Beach Month
- Cataract Awareness Month
- International Youth Day

• September

- Women's Health and Fitness Day
- Family Health and Fitness Day
- Labor Day
- Fall
- Prostate Cancer Awareness Month
- Baby Safety Month
- Ovarian Cancer Awareness Month
- Food Safety Education Month
- Attention Deficit Hyperactivity Disorder (ADHD) Month
- Emergency Preparedness Month
- College Savings Month
- Waffle Week
- International Literacy Day
- Grandparents Day
- Patriot Day
- Healthcare Environmental Services Week

  - World Heart Day
  - International Day of Peace
  - NFL starts
- October
  - Children's Health Day
  - Boss Day
  - Halloween
  - Mother-in-Law Day
  - Medical Librarian's Month
  - Breast Cancer Awareness Month
  - Physical Therapy Month
  - Disability Awareness Month
  - Bone and Joint Awareness Week
  - Dental Hygiene Month
  - Book Month
  - Dyslexia Awareness Month
  - Fire Prevention Week
  - Columbus Day
  - World Food Day
  - Health Education Week
  - Red Ribbon Week
  - United Nations Day
- November
  - American Diabetes Month
  - Thanksgiving

Download this **Content Calendar** by visiting *http://ilink.me/12months*

- o Black Friday
- o Cyber Month and Cyber Monday
- o Lung Cancer Awareness Month
- o Epilepsy Awareness Month
- o Alzheimer's Disease Month
- o Home Care & Hospice Month
- o Veterans Day
- o Youth Appreciation Week
- o Family Week

- December
  - o Hanukkah
  - o Christmas
  - o Safe Toys and Gifts Month
  - o Holidays
  - o AIDs Awareness Month
  - o Read a New Book Month
  - o Seasonal Depression Awareness Month
  - o Human Rights Week
  - o New Year's Eve

Getting Started

With all of this work and planning under your belt, the final phase of your marketing plan is laying out your execution strategy, including a start-up plan. Your plan should be detailed and specific, and you should assign responsibility and accountability for each element of the plan. You must also put processes in place to monitor progress on the plan. Incorporated in this is a frequent (at least monthly) review of the metrics you have established to measure your progress and success. If you are not meeting expectations with those metrics, take the time to recalibrate. What is causing the shortfall? What else can be done to gain more visibility, subscribers, and visitors? Look to whatever metric is falling short. This is an ongoing process—a journey, not a trip to the grocery store. Make sure you are prepared to invest the necessary resources, either internally or with an outsourced partner. However you choose to proceed, you—the owner/leader/key executive/CMO of the company—must be fully engaged. Much can be delegated, but the overall responsibility and accountability is yours and yours alone.

So here is an example of a start-up execution plan:

- **Week 1**
  - o Kick-Off Meeting with Team (internal and external resources, as appropriate)
  - o Confirm All Capabilities for Website (either starting from ground up if—heaven forbid—you don't have a website, or refreshing/rewriting your current web content. Keep in mind a mobile-first strategy. It may be time to start from scratch on a re-do of your site.)
  - o Build & Confirm Social Media Resource Library
    - Informational news sources, keywords, target audiences
    - Content distribution strategy
  - o Find & Test Plug-Ins for Website
  - o Explore and Present 3 Website Themes
  - o Build and Confirm Site Map
- **Week 2**
  - o Build Social Sites with Branded URL
  - o Build Contact Sources
  - o Add Site Map and Plug Ins to Website
  - o Create and Present 3 Logos (if you plan to change your logo or don't have one yet)
  - o Purchase Domain name with Email (assuming you don't already have this in place)

- **Week 3**
  - o Decide on Logos (optional)
  - o Build Branding Mock Ups for the Social Sites
  - o Add in All Copy for Website
  - o Confirm and Add Final Branding to Social Sites
  - o Test and Launch Website
  - o Install Google Analytics
  - o Begin Social Media Soft Launch after Website Launch
- **Week 4**
  - o Confirm and Add Final Branding to Social Sites
  - o Test and Launch Website
  - o Install Google Analytics
  - o Begin Social Media Soft Launch after Website Launch
  - o Initiate Public Relations plan (this will link back to your master marketing plan)
- **After**
  - o Consistent updating and monitoring of sites from this point forward
  - o Monthly Team Meeting to review past month's analytics, upcoming news and events, and to generate recommendations to enhance online marketing efforts
  - o Actively find and engage with new audience members on social networks

Public Relations

As I have indicated, your public relations strategy should be part of your master marketing plan, but may have added elements related to your untethered marketing strategy. Here are a few PR strategies and tactics you can consider, both for your master plan and your untethered marketing plan:

- Create a media kit:
    - Put together materials in both print and electronic form to have on hand when pitching stories
        - Company fact sheet
        - Biographies and head shots of executives and key players
        - Photos – include company logo, product shots, etc.
        - Customer testimonials
        - Latest news in the form of press releases, news blurbs, etc
        - Brochures and other sales materials
        - List of suggested questions
- Create a media list:
    - A media list of bloggers, writers, editors, and publications in areas relevant to your business should be created and maintained. You and/or your agency must then build relationships and pitch story ideas to these media professionals.
- Facebook Advertising Campaigns:
    - This can be created around quarterly promotions. Creative ads can link to your website and/or your Facebook company page. You will want to test different images and calls to action to see what gets those click-thrus.
- Blogger/Writer Outreach Program:
    - A blogger/writer outreach program should be developed. This includes targeting bloggers and writers to sample your products/services. Through this program, a blogger/writer event can be hosted or products can be shipped to the individual.
- Events
    - Research tradeshows and events relevant to your industry

Chapter Eight: Where Do We Go From Here?

I don't claim to have a crystal ball that will tell us what is coming in the future. There will be obvious things, and there will be many, many unexpected things. The key is to have an open mind, monitor trends and announcements, and look for ways to engage, promote, leverage … and bring to market new products and services that do the same.

Several things are clear: The speed and bandwidth for mobile communications and wireless networking in general will only get faster. Battery life on devices will get better. Screens will be thinner and device weights will be lower. Mobile devices will be able to project full-size images. More things will move to the cloud. NFC will come to fruition, with more "wallet" apps and the ability to pay right from your mobile device. Augmented reality will improve and become more mainstream.

Mobile devices will do more. For many users, mobile devices will be the center of their home entertainment world and more. They will control your entertainment devices, security systems, environmental conditions—the possibilities are endless. What this means to you as a marketer is that these mobile devices will be perpetually in the hands and pockets of an increasing number of users, who will grow increasingly dependent on them and expect to be able to do more with them. Be sure you are positioned to take advantage of this evolving trend. Don't be left out!

In terms of the cloud, there will be more providers, lower prices, better and more diverse services. It is the same thing that happened in the data center world and it will happen with the cloud as well.

Untethering Education

You should also keep an eye on what is happening in your local schools—as a parent, but also with the view that these students are your future customers. What devices are they using, how is mobile being integrated into the educational experience—or not? Maybe you can help modernize a local school or district.

I live in Wilmington, Massachusetts, right in the midst of the Route 128 technology hub, our own Silicon Valley. In 2000,I was shocked that our teachers were not connected in the classroom! So I did something about it. I put together a Net Day for the school, rounded up volunteers and donations, hand-wired the school, and worked with the town to get cable services. This motivated the IT department for the district to conduct similar Net days for the rest of the district. I like to think this made/is making a huge difference for our schools and our future employees and customers. It will also better prepare students for success in college.

Don't assume your schools are already on-board with this. In fact, expect resistance. Some stakeholders will support an effort like this, some won't. But be persistent. Sometimes our technology is far ahead of what the schools can do. I should be able to go online to see whether my kid turned in his homework, or what his homework for tonight is. I should be able to easily contact and chat with teachers to monitor progress, and in turn, they should be able to more easily contact me to alert me to issues and concerns.

Many schools have a no-cell-phone policy, but many are beginning to realize that this policy eliminates tools that can enhance communication and the educational experience, so some schools are reevaluating the policy and trying to find a compromise that will benefit everyone. Get involved in these discussions.

Be an Agent of Change

As a citizen of this untethered future, stop trying to protect the old model - in your business, your community, your schools, your libraries, and your town. Will our libraries still be the same two, three, four years down the road? Do we downsize the libraries? Will printed content dominate libraries of the future? How will the way people access content change? How will the way our students learn and our teachers teach, change? For all of this surely will change. Do we need a post office in every town? Once you start questioning the "old ways," the questions keep coming.

Be engaged. Help drive the change, don't hold it back. The work you are doing to develop an untethered business model puts you squarely on the leading edge of these changes. Take advantage of that—for social good, for the good of your business, community, employees, and especially your customers. Pick a project your team can engage in. Not only will you contribute to your community, but you will build loyalty, pride and excitement among your employees, and have great stories to share with the press and with your customers/prospects.

Chapter Nine: Wrapping It Up

So here we are, at the end of the book. Well, not really. Remember that this is a virtual book - an evergreen book - and we will be updating information on our resource page as we move forward. And because we print these books on demand (or deliver them as ebooks), we can have new editions once a week, once a month, once a year, whenever it makes sense. And we will do that.

Our resource page also has a number of tools you can use as you make the transition to an untethered business. Take advantage of them.

This is an exciting journey, and we are just at the beginning of a cycle of massive change. I hope you are on board with me and this concept after reading this book. If not, please let me know, because I haven't done my job!

If you are on board, keep me posted on your progress. I would love to publish your story on our resource page and blog about your success!

We truly live in an untethered world, and far too many businesses are still stuck in a static, tethered environment that is not nearly nimble, flexible or visible enough to be successful in today's dynamic world.

My goal with this book was to educate you about cloud computing and mobile communications; to give you ideas about how you can use these concepts to revolutionize your business; and to give you concrete, actionable ideas that will allow you to move forward rapidly. I believe that has been accomplished, but you—the reader, the business person—are the ultimate arbiter.

So go forth and untether. We'll be right there with you. It's a lot of hard work, but that work is fun and exciting. And the rewards are there for those who believe. Scan the QR Code below to contact me with your Marketing questions.